500 ways

to Beat the Hollywood Script Reader

★ ★ ★

Writing the Screenplay the Reader Will Recommend

Jennifer Lerch

Fireside • Published by Simon & Schuster

To My Redeemer

FIRESIDE
Rockefeller Center
1230 Avenue of the Americas
New York, NY 10020

Copyright © 1999 by Jennifer Lerch
All rights reserved,
including the right of reproduction
in whole or in part in any form.

FIRESIDE and colophon are registered trademarks
of Simon & Schuster Inc.

Designed by Pei Loi Koay

Manufactured in the United States of America

10   9   8   7   6   5   4   3

Library of Congress Cataloging-in-Publication Data
Lerch, Jennifer.
    500 ways to beat the Hollywood script reader : writing the
screenplay the reader will recommend / Jennifer Lerch.
        p.   cm.
    1. Motion picture authorship.   2. Motion picture plays—
Technique.   I. Title.   II. Title: Five hundred ways to beat the
Hollywood script reader.
PN1996.L43   1999
808.2'3—dc21   99-25212
                                                    CIP

ISBN 0-684-85640-9 (pbk.)

Acknowledgments

Like all Hollywood productions, this book is a fusion of many talents. These are the gifted players whose gracious help made *500 Ways* happen:

Adam Novak, the Story Department Head at the William Morris Agency in Beverly Hills, who pitched the project, then tirelessly supplied and refined some of the most colorful tips and examples. His fingerprints appear on almost every page of this book. The gong, the bridge, The Arch Deluxe—read the book and you'll know what I'm talking about.

Marcy Posner, the William Morris agent who ran with this project as soon as it rolled out of the printer and sold it to the best publisher in the world. You're truly a writer's best friend.

Caroline Sutton, the gifted senior editor at Fireside Books whose patience, gentle hand, and belief in the project allowed the book to become as good as it could be.

Patti Carr, who contributed tips and edited a preliminary manuscript while moving up the Hollywood ladder from Hollywood Reader to sitcom writer. Patti even put her husband, Rob, to work, and he came up with a tip or two, too!

David Dorfman, whose tips are some of the best in the book. And this is a guy who knows what he's talking about—David went from freelance script reader to million-dollar screenwriter overnight (give or take a year or two or ten) by putting his knowledge of beating the Hollywood Reader to work for himself!

Aaron Shershow, a Hollywood Reader turned producer, who offered pages of valuable tips, funny examples, and some great anecdotes, too.

Liz Brixius, a talented screenwriter, who shared great tips related to Acts 1 and 2.

Dorothy Eustis Lerch, my mystery-reading mom, who provided tips without even being asked!

Dr. Jerry Lerch, my orthodontist dad, who performed an excruciatingly tedious preliminary edit.

Mark Cole, who helped to originate the concept.

Jan and Bernie Budnik, whose initial excitement about the concept got this writer off and running, and whose vigilance kept the baddies away.

Lucille Chaney, the lady who stood between heaven and hell on behalf of me and this project most every day since it began. My deepest thanks to you.

Contents

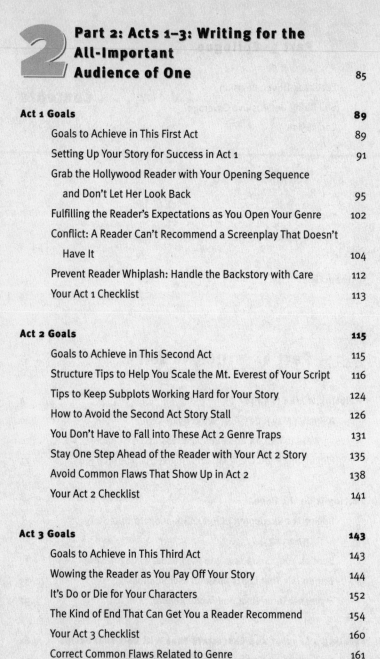

2 Part 2: Acts 1–3: Writing for the All-Important Audience of One

3 Part 3: Epilogue

Introduction

Have you ever gone to a movie and thought, *I could write something better than that?*

Let's say you *do* write a screenplay. When you send it to a talent agency, production company, or movie studio, it will land on the desk of a Hollywood Reader. This Hollywood Reader is often the first and only person to make a decision about whether or not your screenplay is something the company should consider.

Why do Hollywood Readers get to make these big decisions?

Hollywood movie studios and production companies receive tens of thousands of screenplays each year, and executives cannot read them all. So the film industry uses Hollywood Readers to sift through the screenplays in search of those that measure up to their standards and offer the elements they're looking for.

Meet the Hollywood Reader

★ ★

The average Hollywood Reader is college educated, culturally savvy, and often has excellent writing skills of her own. Most important, the Hollywood Reader has a proven track record of knowing what screenplay concepts, stories, and characters click with executives, what elite acting talent would give their eye teeth to be in on, and what hits a nerve with audiences. The Hollywood Reader also knows how to communicate all the essential points about the screenplay to the executive in a brief, insightful document that the Industry calls coverage.

Coverage

★ ★

Think cheat sheet when you think coverage. It's the unofficial Cliffs Notes *version of your screenplay. And more people in Hollywood read the cheat sheet than read the original document (your screenplay).*

That's a scary thought for any screenwriter. But it can be less frightening if you know what the Hollywood Reader looks for when evaluating your screenplay—because then you can make those areas as strong as possible so the reader gives positive comments in the coverage.

Unclear about what coverage looks like? Let's explore it.

The Anatomy of Coverage

The Hollywood Reader's coverage report usually has four parts: a concept line(s), a synopsis, a comments page, and a graph.

- The *concept* sums up your story in a sentence or two.
- The *synopsis* details your screenplay's story line in several paragraphs or pages.
- The *comments* page analyzes the screenplay's strengths and weaknesses, compares it to existing films, and offers a bottom-line opinion about whether the company should consider buying, producing, or casting clients in your project.
- The *graph* shows the executive at a glance where your characters, story, dialogue, and structure rate. One such graph looks like this:

	EXCELLENT	GOOD	FAIR	POOR
CHARACTERS				
DIALOGUE				
PLOT				
STRUCTURE				

Recommend _____   Consider _____   Pass _____

If the Coverage Is Positive

If the coverage intrigues the executive because of the comments or story idea, she *may* begin reading your screenplay. If the screenplay delivers on the Hollywood Reader's promises, that executive may decide to option or buy your screenplay or (in the case of a talent agency) represent it or recommend it to a client.

A Trade Secret

A not-so-well-kept secret among Hollywood insiders is that an executive may buy your screenplay *without even reading it.* Her thoughts about your screenplay will be based solely on the Hollywood Reader's coverage. In fact, Hollywood executives daily discuss screenplays over the phone by reading from coverage. Both parties know what's going on. The person who "wins" in the conversation is the executive who has the better coverage. That's the importance of getting good coverage.

This Book Can Help You Get Better Coverage

★ ★

No other book demystifies the work of the Hollywood Reader by exposing the nitty-gritty elements the pros look for when evaluating your work. Each page offers the inside information you need in order to write a screenplay that can make it to the executive's desk with glowing coverage. Tips on everything from concept to story to structure, characters, dialogue, pacing, and more are arranged in an easy-to-use format that covers the essentials of writing a screenplay, cover-to-cover.

These tips apply to most stories and address the flaws that most often undercut a writer's work. To prevent the complication of cross-referencing, some tips are repeated with the intention of making the book as easy as possible to use.

Bottom line: The information contained in these pages is as universal and fail-safe as you're going to find. If it's not included in this book, chances are you probably don't need to do it!

What the Hollywood Reader *Wants* to Do with Your Script

★ ★

Every script reader in today's Hollywood wants to be the one to bring her boss the next Academy Award winner, the project that will draw top talent, the screen story that will define a generation—the best script around. And any reader worth her salt knows that searching for great scripts is like mining diamonds: You've got to know how to spot potential and grab it when you see it, because most scripts don't have an immediate sparkle. Some do. But most do not.

That's not a slam on screenwriters, some of whom are incredibly gifted. It's reality. And that reality benefits you. How?

A Script Doesn't Need to Be Perfect

★ ★

A script does not need to be perfect in order to sell in today's Hollywood. Each script has its own reasons for selling—sometimes it features an original character or a unique, catchy concept that grabs a studio executive who has visions of a snappy one-sheet (a movie poster). A script might have the breezy dialogue that gets beneath the skin of its characters. Or the story line may hit a timely note. It could be that a script happens to fit *the genre a studio is trying to fill on its production slate. The script could catch the fancy of a gifted talent agent who has the ability to sell* anything, *and who often* does *sell anything on any given day in Hollywood.*

The point: A script doesn't need to be anywhere near perfect to sell in Hollywood's marketplace. Some scripts are AMAZING. Most are not. And that's great news if you're a screenwriter. All you've got to do is write a script that can get you great coverage from the Hollywood Reader.

What a Reader Looks For

★ ★

This book shows you what a script reader looks for when evaluating a screenplay. It alerts you to common flaws in screenplays and provides ways in which you can correct some of these flaws and strengthen just about any project.

Not every tip applies to every script. But many of the tips can be applied to most scripts.

The Readers Who Contributed to This Book

★ ★

Each tip has been reviewed by working Hollywood Readers who don't have an ax to grind.

Do these readers know anything about screenwriting? Well, during the process of writing this book, two of the contributors became working screenwriters. One reader became a staff writer on a popular network television show, and another received a screenwriting contract worth more than $1 million and is scripting comedy features for premier directors in addition to his contract. Another reader has since become an employed producer. Yet another reader is a respected story executive.

These people know what they're talking about.

And these readers typify the person who will read your script:

people who are interested in building careers in entertainment. People like you.

So Relax

* *

This book attempts to put your mind at ease about the Hollywood Reader by walking you through the process of what a reader may look for when evaluating a project. The scripts written by the top writers do almost all of the things covered in this book. That's what you want to shoot for: doing as much as you can to craft a screenplay that is beyond reproach.

This book exists ultimately for one purpose: to help you move into the ranks of working screenwriters. The information comes from the point of view of someone involved in the sales process. That someone may be a reader, but that reader is a person. An audience. An audience of one to which your screen story must play as if it's unfolding on a movie screen. And this audience isn't looking for anything more than the audience down at the neighborhood multiplex looks for. She wants to be entertained, to experience life through someone else's eyes, to grow through a dramatic experience.

Play to this audience of one. Write with passion, humor, honesty, and always with imagination.

Chances are, the Hollywood Reader wants to recommend some project this week. Make that project be yours.

Part 1

* * *

Writing to Sell

Scripting It Like the Pros Do

Like every other industry on the planet, Hollywood has its standards. This is especially true when it comes to the screenplay. Either a screenwriter conforms her work to industry standards or she doesn't. If she doesn't, she tips off the reader that she is unfamiliar with screenwriting in general and that her work will probably have significant problems with character, story, and structure.

Does this seem like a leap from style to substance?

It might, except that because screenwriting does not have dozens of nitpicky, exacting little rules, the professional screenwriter conforms to the few, basic requirements and hands in a fairly standardized document.

What can you standardize?

Dialogue margins (buy software for screenwriters and get your margins right), the amount of verbiage given to describing characters and detailing action, and screenplay length (100 to 120 pages). These are things that almost anyone familiar with screenwriting can see up front. Other areas that a savvy, seasoned reader can spot immediately is the flow of good dialogue—she knows what realistic dialogue looks like on the page.

Never seen a screenplay and live outside of Los Angeles?

Published screenplays are increasingly plentiful in writer's bookstores. Study these scripts and you'll see how top screenwriters put their stories on the page.

A Reader May Judge Your Script by Its Cover

★ ★

There's no getting around it: Looks matter in today's Hollywood.

Does this talk of appearance sound superficial? It's not. Most top screenplays have a certain look that a reader worth her salt cues into. And this look is obtainable if you sidestep the flaws detailed in the following tips.

These tips address the relatively easy stuff. Get the cover and first few pages of your script right, and you're on your way to beating the Hollywood script reader.

23 Ways to Make a Good First Impression on a Reader

★ ★

Before reading your script, a Hollywood Reader can decide if you're a pro by checking your writing credits. But it's much more efficient to glance at your script's general appearance, read the cover, and flip through its pages. And often it's just as revealing.

Sound ruthless or unfair? If a writer doesn't have some of the basic mechanics of the craft down, chances are that she's making more serious mistakes in the script's content as well.

Even if you've just written one script, don't allow the reader to begin building a case against it before she gets into the story. Do yourself and the project a favor by taking these tips.

Jennifer Lerch

General Overall Appearance

1 Screenplays that *look* professional usually *are* professional. Consider your screenplay as your calling card. Send out nothing less than crisp, clean copies of it. Coffee stains, handwritten notes, information that's been scratched out—these things don't belong on your cover. Clean disfiguring marks off your script before copying it. What reader wants to recommend to her boss a script that looks like it belongs in the garbage? What executive wants to read a script that looks like it belongs in the garbage? Crisp, clean copies. Always.

2 Use high-quality white copy paper for the cover and the rest of the screenplay. Onion skin, paper heavier than 20 pound, erasable paper, and colored paper telegraph amateurism. Yes, all of these have crossed my desk at one time or another.

3 Keep your script svelte: 100 to 120 pages. Feature screenplays that are significantly fatter (or thinner) mark a screenplay as unprofessional. An experienced Hollywood Reader can often gauge a script's page count by its thickness even before picking it up and looking at the page numbers.

Professional Binding

4 Bind your screenplay with two or three strong brads to ensure that it stays together. Cheap brads or brads that are too small or too thin won't hold the screenplay pages together when it's read. The screenplay that falls apart physically usually also falls apart in terms of story and structure. Keep every part of your script together. Use strong brads.

5 Legal bindings, notebooks, velo and spiral bindings look amateur and make photocopying difficult. The pros don't use these and neither should you.

The Cover

6 Use your screenplay's cover for written information only. The screenplay's title, your name, phone number, and possibly your address are all that's needed on this page. If you have an agent, the agent's name and phone number should appear in place of your phone number and address. A professional screenplay cover looks like this:

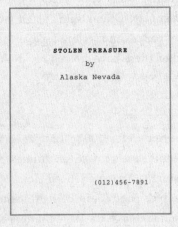

```
                    STOLEN TREASURE
                          by
                    Alaska Nevada




                    (012)456-7891
```

7 The print font most used on Hollywood screenplay covers is twelve point Courier bold. A font that is larger, smaller, or fancier telegraphs amateurism. Nonprofessional screenwriters will often blow up the type size. That's a mistake. Exaggerating a font for the title draws negative attention. Capitalizing the title is enough in today's Hollywood.

8 Get a Los Angeles phone number and voice mail if you have not made the commitment of a move to the city. Most legitimate Hollywood screenwriters, producers, and agents live in Los Angeles. An out-of-town address or phone number on the screenplay cover can be a red flag to some readers, indicating that the author has yet to get serious about her craft and make the move to the entertainment capital of the world. Sounds like an odd note, but seasoned readers know this to be true.

9 Delete draft dates and draft numbers from your spec script's cover. If your screenplay has been floating around town for ten years, you don't want to advertise this. Let the Hollywood Reader make her decision based on the screenplay's contents, not on its history.

10 Author's labels warning "No copying or coverage without permission of the author or the author's representative" scream amateur. Not only does paranoia turn off industry insiders, but it's impossible to move a project smoothly while strictly adhering to it. Movie studios and production companies can place warning statements on your work, but if you are new to the industry, have no representation or production deals, and are in the stage of getting people interested in your project, get used to the idea that your project *has* to endure handling before it gets into the hands of the person(s) with the authority to make a final decision.

11 Resist the temptation to put a graphic on the cover. Better to save your creativity for the screenplay's characters, story, and dialogue. In the nearly 10,000 projects I've covered, only one professional writer included a drawing on his script's cover. And he's well known in the industry. Are you?

12 Only have a dot matrix printer? Print your script on a friend's ink-jet or laser printer, or at the copy shop. Dot matrix is hard on the eyes and generally nonstandard. Anything that is nonstandard is a red flag you can do without.

Beyond the Cover

13 After the cover page, most professional screenplays begin on page 1 of the screenplay's text. Including other information between the cover and page 1 risks raising a red flag.

14 An exception to the above tip is an epigraph that follows on a separate page. The best epigraphs are short, relevant, and to the point. A brief quote or quotes that relate to your story's theme is the norm if you choose to include an epigraph.

15 Tempted to include a résumé and film budget? Resist, unless the executive requests these elements.

16 Want to include a sheet listing your dream cast? There's a more professional way to interest top talent in your project: Send the script to the star's agent, manager, or production company. A dream cast is a tip-off that you're still in the dreaming phase of your career and not yet in the reality-based doing phase of the business. Learn how the Hollywood system works and go through the proper channels. There are so few standards in the industry, it just makes good sense to conform to them.

Eliminating Page 1, 2, 3 Tip-offs That You're Not Yet a Pro

★ ★

These tips show you how to correct the flaws that appear in most amateur screenplays but which never seem to surface in professional screenplays. The savvy, experienced Hollywood Reader picks up on these missteps in seconds, and the writer instantly begins losing credibility.

Why? Usually these flaws are just the tip of the iceberg— serious story and character flaws almost always appear in the ensuing pages. Get it right from the top and you create a more level playing field for yourself, even if you've never before sold a screenplay. Write like a professional and one day you will be a professional.

Page 1

17 Eliminate flowery language. If the script opens on black, write BLACK and not *We open on deep, dark black that oozes evil.* The single word BLACK communicates much more than just the absence of light. It communicates that you understand the power of language and the craft of screenwriting. For more tips on screenwriting style that screams *Professional!* to the Hollywood Reader, turn to *Style That Turns On a Hollywood Reader* (page 52).

18 Describe the characters who participate in the scenes. A character without description is a black hole that talks—who knows *what's* talking! Rather than leaving the reader to fill in the blanks for herself, only to find that her ideas conflict with your vision later in the story, communicate your thoughts about the character in a few succinct phrases. For more tips on describing your characters, turn to *Burning Your Characters into the Reader's Imagination* (page 34).

19 Give your action moves that will excite the Hollywood Reader. Describing pointless, unimportant, or obvious action like *Rob gets in the car and drives away* telegraphs *Amateur!* Eliminating such scenes instantly brings your script up a notch or two in the eyes of the Hollywood Reader. For more tips on scripting action that gets the reader's adrenaline pumping, turn to *Style That Turns On a Hollywood Reader* (page 52) as well as tips 330–348.

20 Use new sluglines each time you change locations so the reader can follow the action. A character who shops in a convenience store then steps into an open manhole in the next line will frustrate the reader (unless the manhole is in the convenience store), giving her the impression that your action is disjointed and you have problems visualizing the scene.

21 If the character doesn't say it, wear it, or do it, delete it. The camera cannot capture detailed thoughts the characters have unless you script them in action and dialogue. A hallmark of amateur writing is including information that the camera cannot capture on screen.

22 In the same vein as the previous tip, description which the camera can't capture will be impossible to convey to the audience. If bodies are buried six feet below where Officer Coreman stands and you want the audience to know this in the first scene, find a way to show it with a physical marker that the audience can read. Screenplays that show no understanding of the relationship between what's on the page and what the camera will capture instantly flag themselves as sub-standard.

23 Thinking of shrinking the type or stretching the dialogue margins to accommodate your too-long feature screenplay in 100 to 120 pages? Think again if you want the reader to take your project seriously. Small type, wide margins, and extra-long paper all telegraph desperation. Get a software program for screenwriting and conform your feature screenplay to industry standards. A few pages over 120 is okay, but once you get into the 130s and 140s your project is suspect.

Putting It on the Page

You've got it in your head, in your notes, in your mouth when you talk about your project with friends and execs. But the typical Hollywood Reader only sees your script—she can't read your mind, see your notes, or hear your pitch. The only way she understands the story you're trying to tell is through the screenplay itself.

You need to get that vision onto the pages of your screenplay in a way that communicates professionally, with color, and with vigor if the Hollywood Reader is to experience the excitement and drama of your story and give your project the coverage it deserves.

The following sections address what you need to know before the reader sees page 1 of your screenplay. We'll explore how to put your screenplay's setting, characters, and dialogue on the page in the most effective way, and conclude the section with a chapter on the writing style that best presents your ideas.

Learn how to communicate your ideas in a way that every reader in Hollywood will appreciate, from the professional reader to the executive, the studio head, the star, the director. The more you can integrate these basic tips into your work, the greater your chances of showing that you understand what screenwriting is all about.

Communicating with professionalism is the name of the

game when it comes to instilling confidence in the people who will spend thousands or possibly millions of dollars buying your project, then invest millions bringing it to the screen.

These tips can help you to communicate in your screenplay with a confidence that says *I know what I'm doing and I'm doing it well.*

Pulling the Reader out of Her Office and into Your Story with Setting

★ ★

The first thing the reader sees on page 1 of your script is the story's setting. Often the way in which you script the setting can tip off the reader to whether or not you understand some fundamentals about the screenwriting craft.

Think of it this way: The way in which you describe your setting is almost as important as the setting itself. If you leave out important details like It's the 13th century, *the Hollywood Reader may wonder why the characters ride horses and live in castles. When you fail to give the Hollywood Reader the information she needs to understand what you hope to convey on the screen, your mistakes eclipse the story and characters. And when this happens, chances are that a reader recommendation is slipping away.*

These tips show how, with a few well-thought-out details related to setting, you can pull the reader out of her office and into your story.

Anchor Your Story with a Setting

24 In the opening scene of your script, you must tell the reader when and where the story takes place to establish the setting in her mind. Remember, the reader doesn't have the benefit of the *seeing* the backdrop or picking up the story's era from the costumes the actors wear. You can convey information related to the setting in the *slugline* that kicks open the door to each scene.

```
EXT. JEROME, ARIZONA -- DAY  1895
```

25 In the opening of your script, when the reader's mind is a blank slate because she knows nothing about your story, adding a brief line or two of description immediately following the slugline can communicate the milieu. The audience will pick up on this through the music, opening credits, lighting, and the director's style, but the Hollywood Reader will understand this only if you tell her.

```
EXT. JEROME, ARIZONA -- DAY  1895


Dusty, bawdy, temporary. A hillside mining town
where everyone gets rich or dies trying.
```

26 Specifying the month in the opening description can convey loads of information about the story's mood to the Hollywood Reader. August in New York City is much different than January in New York City. If you choose to include a month as a detail, make it into an integral part of your story so that your script seems less haphazard, more organic. Make every detail count for something in your story.

Special Note for Unfamiliar Historical Settings

27 A story set in a long-gone historical era needs more detail than a story set in the modern world, especially if the era has not been popularized by recent entertainment. Establish the setting by grounding the details about the setting in actual history.

```
1350, Northern Europe. The Black Plague claims a
third of the population, gunpowder emerges, serfdom
declines.
```

Think of establishing a historical setting as giving a miniature history lesson with an eye toward using the details provided here later in your story.

28 When you create a historical setting, give special attention to establishing the milieu—the social and cultural environment—so that the reader understands the characters' values, fears, and ultimately the impetus of your characters as they stretch and grow during your story. A comment like *Necklines are as high as the morals* communicates that the characters probably don't sleep around openly.

29 Brevity is a strength when establishing a historical setting, but avoid writing something like *Think Braveheart*. Mentioning another film can flood the Hollywood Reader's mind with possibly erroneous details and cause unwanted comparisons to your story. Your story is your time to shine.

A Story Set in the Future

30 If your story is set in the future, assign a specific year date so the Hollywood Reader can be prepared for the changes in transportation, politics, and more. A setting in 4500 needs more detailing than a setting in 2015.

When you must go into detail to describe a radically different setting, edit the amount of exposition needed to set up the story. You can do this by finding ways to *show* what's different through the characters' action and interaction instead of writing paragraphs of novelish exposition. Your story will translate with more impact to the screen if you do this, because the audience will see the changes in action.

For example, if the system of government has radically changed, show the government functioning (a financially bankrupt character being carted off to the work farm, for example) so we get a vivid, dramatic picture of the milieu you have in mind.

A Story Set in an Obscure Location

31 When you set your story in a location that may not be well known to the general public, briefly describe the scene so that a Hollywood Reader can capture your vision.

This tip is especially useful if you create a fictional setting for your story. Writing something like *Hometown, USA, where Mom, July 4 fireworks, and the annual pie-eating contest rank as the most important things in life* communicates volumes to the Hollywood Reader about a happy, homespun environment.

Is the Setting Working Hard Enough for Your Story?

A good setting does more than provide a place to play out a scene. A setting worth more than the paper it's printed on works hard for your characters and story, taking on a life of its own as it plays an integral role in the action.

The following five tips show you how to impress a reader with this element that so many writers seem to throw away.

32 The setting you choose should be the *only* place your story can play out—your story won't make sense if it's set anywhere else. That's how big a part of your screenplay the setting should be.

33 The more unique the setting, the greater your chance of pulling the Hollywood Reader into the screenplay in the opening slugline. Compare a story that opens in a magical Sahara Desert oasis with a story that opens on city streets. You've immediately grabbed the reader's full attention with your oasis setting. Best of all, because few stories are set in a desert oasis, the reader's mind isn't flooded instantly with other stories that she inevitably compares with yours. You're off to a great start.

34 Choose a setting that will enhance and add texture to your story. A standard romance set against the backdrop of a revolution has more potential for drama than a romance set in a sleepy town. If your setting doesn't contribute to your story, find a setting that does.

35 Choose a setting that will aggravate your protagonist's problems. Give your protagonist a fear of animals and set your story in the wilds of Africa. Make the setting work for you by working *against* your lead character. With most scripts suffering from a lack of conflict, the more ways that you find to integrate conflict into your screenplay, the stronger the screenplay will be.

500 Ways to Beat the Hollywood Script Reader

36 Use the setting as an opportunity to create plot twists and obstacles that your characters must overcome to achieve their goals. If you set your story during a blustery Connecticut winter, make the cold, wet, dark days and snowstorms inform the action and the characters' choices, moods, and even their goals. But as you do this, find unique ways to use the snowstorms, the darkness, and the cold so you don't have the reader predicting that the two characters who love to hate each other will get trapped by the snowstorm and admit their true, amorous feelings for each other.

Burning Your Characters into the Reader's Imagination

* *

No matter how hard a Hollywood Reader tries, she will rarely see the characters in the same way you do. Including the right details is essential to communicating your vision in the screenplay and bringing the characters to life. Without the benefit of flesh-and-blood people portraying the personalities on the screen, the reader is left to use her imagination to fill in the important character-related blanks in your screenplay. Don't leave any important blanks for the Hollywood Reader (or the actor or the director) to fill in. Imprint your vision on the page in such a way that it sears the reader's imagination, making your intentions unmistakable.

Scripting your characters right is worth any extra effort it may take: The projects that feature unforgettable personalities are often the projects that get recommended.

Introducing Your Characters

37 Every character needs an introduction, but reserve more involved descriptions for major characters and major scenes.

This cues the Hollywood Reader in to who is a major character and who is a face in the crowd. A more involved description might include details about clothing, body type, hair style, the look in the eyes. Compare the minimal descriptions of

Gary Silver, 35, smarmy

with

Jack Moore, 35—even the wrinkled oxford, worn Levi's, and tousled hair can't play down his charm

38 No matter how small a role a character plays, assign each of your characters with an age the first time he or she appears in your story so the Hollywood Reader is able to see that character through your eyes and understand his or her on-screen choices and action.

Sandy, mid-20s

Vicky, 94

Unless we know Vicky is ninety-four, we're going to wonder why she's in a wheelchair or why she moves slowly. Including the right details is key to keeping the reader's mind on the action and into your story.

Describing Physical Traits

39 Define a few salient physical traits when describing your character for the first time so the Hollywood Reader forms a mental picture. Since this mental picture is unlikely to change as the screenplay progresses, choose a few vivid details and communicate them clearly so that your characters will be represented with accuracy in the Hollywood Reader's coverage.

Jinx Paige, a panther in Armani

Sully Dylan, a fireplug of a man

Jill Weston, Einstein brain in a Miss Universe body

40 Keep the description general enough so that it captures the personality you want to express, but leave the details about the physical type open to interpretation. You're not going to turn down the trim brunette superstar who may be interested in playing the role you wrote for a buxom blonde. The exception to this tip is a story in which roles go against type (the blonde cheerleader who scores a perfect 1600 on her SAT).

41 While you want to keep details related to physical description general, you do want to be mindful that the words you use to describe your characters' *movements* convey volumes about their build, emotional attitude, and mental alacrity. Does your character glide, waddle, or schlep into a room? Figure it out and put it into your script to create a character who comes to life in the reader's imagination.

Give Your Characters Jobs

42 Showing what a character does for a living isn't always necessary and may not come into play in each story, but this information often supplies significant details about characters—their talents, their frustrations, the challenges they face, how they spend their time. A job title can be a simple way to communicate a great deal of information about a character to a Hollywood Reader. *BOBBIE, a chorus girl. JOE, a construction worker.* And remember to not fall prey to clichés. Give chorus girl Bobbie some smarts and ambition. Give construction worker Joe a degree in philosophy.

What to Avoid in Character Description

43 Delete actors' names from your screenplay. Specifying who you'd like to play a role risks alienating other actors who may be interested in the same role.

44 Comparing the characters in your story to characters in movies and books is risky—the Hollywood Reader may not be familiar with what you're describing and may miss the point you're trying to make.

45 Screenplays that identify a character as *our trustworthy protagonist* or *the nefarious villain* tip off the Hollywood Reader that the project is probably not tops. Show who the characters are by the things they do. If Billy is smart, show him getting the answer to the math problem before the other kids in the classroom.

Naming Your Characters

46 Assign your characters names that are distinctively different. Scenes featuring two characters who have names like Alan and Alain or Tina and Tia can be misread by a weary or careless Hollywood Reader and make it difficult for her to follow your screenplay. It's to your advantage to make the project as clear and accessible as possible on the page. Also, writers who give their characters names that are similar sometimes confuse the two names and have the same character engaging in a conversation with himself. Do yourself a favor and come up with names that look different in print.

47 If two characters must have the same name, put numbers after the names. For example, *Alice #1, Alice #2, Alice #3*. If your story flashes forward and back in time and features the same character in the different eras, write *Child Alice* and *Adult Alice*. Keep the character's identity as clear as possible with a minimum of description.

48 Providing your characters with a first name and a surname communicates a solid, whole identity. Characters with only one name (unless it's a distinct nickname) telegraphs an incomplete identity.

A Character's Internal Landscape

49 Create internal, private conflicts for each of your characters. Actors vie for the chance to portray characters riddled by doubts, insecurities, unfinished business in relationships with family members and friends. Your characters need not be the walking wounded, but do make them multidimensional so they come across as authentic and complex.

When you do make a character insecure (for example), it's always stronger to show us the insecurity in a dramatic, visual way rather than just including the insecurity in the character description. The character will ultimately be known by what he does and says anyway, so find a way to turn your characters inside out, having them act out who they are throughout the story.

50 Decide on a range of emotion for each character. Does this person get hysterical, remain calm in the most tense situations, shut out painful events, throw things around, flop to the ground and weep, or show nothing at all while under stress? Making these kinds of decisions about each character helps you communicate a more complete personality to the reader (and to the actor who will eventually portray the character on the screen). It's another way of turning your character inside out for the reader and the movie audience.

51 Give each of your characters secrets that will come out in the story to ensure that your story (and your characters) has layers of discovery. Mandy's abortion, Roger's prison term, Lily's fluency in eight languages, Sara's experience as a spy could provide material needed to give your story a twist.

Consistency in Characters

52 Review the decisions you're making about your characters, looking for possible points where your characters contradict themselves in the way they act and the way you've described them. If you describe Jinx Paige as a panther in Armani but then show him struggling to get a date or easily intimidated in business, you're conveying inconsistency that undercuts your character's credibility. Consistency is a hallmark of professional screenwriting.

Screen Talk That Looks as Good as It Sounds
★ ★

When it comes to putting words in your characters' mouths, it's essential to write dialogue that sounds good on the page.

Remember: The reader doesn't have the advantage of hearing a spoken delivery—she picks up the characters' intent, energy, state of heart, and state of mind from the words, phrasing, and punctuation the characters use.

Never seen dialogue scripted on a page? Buy some published screenplays and study them. Each writer has his or her own style, but you'll quickly catch on to the basics.

No matter what your style of writing screen talk, you'll want to take these tips that address the flaws which most often prevent dialogue from talking out loud on the page.

Fresh Dialogue

53 Forget proper English. If the sentences are complete but the exchanges are flat or stiff, you need to let the characters dictate where the commas, periods, and other punctuation marks go. *Color me curious, but do you know anything about . . . bombs?*

54 Every line should sound as though you've taken the words out of the characters' mouths and put them onto the page. That's the key to giving dialogue the flavor of life. Read your lines out loud to see if they sound right.

What Most Undermines Fresh Dialogue?

55 One common criticism is that dialogue is *wooden*—the lines seem dull or stiff. Compare *I will go now, Mother* with *Later, Momsy!* Bring your characters to life with the words they speak. Decide how each character will talk, what mood they're in, their general attitude about life, and the point you're trying to make in the scene. Filling in these blanks about your characters can help you craft dialogue that does its job in your screenplay.

56 Another common criticism: Dialogue is *on the nose*. It states too clearly what the character is thinking without filtering those thoughts through the character's personality and agenda. If sixteen-year-old Megan has a crush on classmate Ben and wants to get to know him, she's not going to go up to him and say *I've got a crush on you*. Chances are she will say something like *Nice shirt* as a way of initiating her agenda of getting to know him better.

57 *Predictable* dialogue undermines some good screenplays. The characters say exactly what characters in other movies and television shows have been saying for decades. One character says, *I love you*. The other character responds, *I love you, too*. You want your dialogue to flow, but you also want it to turn your character inside out for the Hollywood Reader, showing her who this person is on the inside—the temperament, humor, intelligence, uniqueness of thought. Rethink predictable exchanges.

58 Another common criticism: Dialogue is *stilted*. As you choose your characters' vocabulary, guard against using words that are too formal for the characters and their circumstance. Compare *I expect remuneration* with *You bet you're gonna pay!* or *How many Jacksons?* Dialogue should always sound as though it's coming out of somebody's mouth—fresh, snappy, in context, and revealing an attitude behind the words.

59 *Disjoint* dialogue can absolutely ruin a screenplay. Keep your characters on track, following an orderly train of thought throughout an exchange. While characters going on tangents, choosing to ignore remarks made by others, and not completely comprehending the full import of what the other character is saying mark good dialogue, there should be connections between the characters as they interact. Be sure your characters are listening to each other, chewing on the thoughts exchanged, and responding accordingly so that your dialogue works for your screenplay.

60 *Lack of variety* in dialogue exchanges can put a reader to sleep. Use physical gestures as part of the communication process in the dialogue to make the exchanges fresh and realistic. For example, six-year-old Timmy can say *Bye, Mom* and Mom can wink in response—she doesn't need to say *Bye, Timmy*, which can make an exchange seem pat and predictable.

Make Your Characters Distinct

61 Create a specific vocabulary for each character. Characters who use the same words and phrases over and over build unforgettable personalities and convey that you know your characters. A character from the South may say *Y'all*, another character may pepper the phrase *You know?* or *You said it!* throughout his or her speech, while another character may answer *Sure* to just about any question posed. Know your characters and put this knowledge into the words they say.

62 Each character in your story should phrase his thoughts differently and have a unique cadence apparent in the way he speaks. Some characters will speak in complicated sentences, others will mutter only phrases or syllables of words in reply to everything. When you get these details down, you communicate a very solid character identity to your reader. Compare a character who says *The fair! Best display of deep-fried Americana north of the Mason-Dixon!* with one who says *Fair? Hicks!*

63 Some characters will always instigate conversations and have to get the last word, others will be much less verbal and will prefer to never talk. Make your character's dialogue reflect and distinguish the personality you create for him. In a dialogue-driven story where there is little action, the chief element at your disposal for bringing the character to life is the dialogue. Use it for all it's worth by pouring your character's personality into it. Dialogue should conform to character first and foremost.

Phrases

64 With rare exceptions, complete, complex sentences in dialogue are the kiss of death. Keep your characters speaking in phrases rather than complete sentences. Phrases suggest breathing room and come across as more realistic. The historical genre and a highly intellectual character are two exceptions to a tip worth taking.

65 Communicate a character's personality, attitude, and background through the words and phrases he or she says. Compare *Hey, babe!* with *Good morning, Marty.*

66 Make your characters' personalities distinct from the first words they speak.

- If Daisy is southern, show us her accent from the start. *Y'all partyin' tonight?*
- If Jeb is a man of few words, show it every time he comes into a scene. Giving him one-word responses like *Yep* and *Nope* communicates this.

Consistency

67 Keep each of your characters speaking in a consistent way. If your character suddenly changes the way he speaks (unless it's part of your plotline), you risk undermining authenticity and sending out the wrong signals about tensions between characters. If Sheila always says *Hi, Katie!* whenever she sees Kathleen, then suddenly says *Hello, Kathleen,* we're cued in that something is up between these two women.

68 A verbal exchange needs to be greater than the sum of its parts. Include levels of meaning in what your characters say to each other. If Susie tells Rachel that *Strange things are happening* as they watch a solar eclipse, Susie can be referring to her dad recently leaving the family, her brother getting into a car wreck, or a recent strange romantic encounter in addition to the eclipse. The more levels of meaning you convey in your dialogue, the more integrated your screenplay will seem and the more weight your dialogue will have.

Content

69 Consider how fast your characters' minds work and then integrate this into the dialogue. Some characters will put two or three thoughts into an exchange while others won't manage to complete even a single thought. Think this through so you reveal the characters' interiors through the words spoken.

70 Similarly, give your characters language that reflects their life experience. A character with a Ph.D. in English will speak differently than an illiterate hermit who lives off the land. A character born in 1940 will speak differently than a character born in 1980.

Punctuating the Dialogue

71 The clearest way to communicate to the Hollywood Reader that characters step on each other's lines is with a double hyphen (--). In this example, a husband and wife are together in a car. The wife holds the map, the husband is hungry and driving.

```
          HUSBAND
I'm hungry.


          WIFE
We missed the--


          HUSBAND
You think there's a McDonald's or--


          WIFE
Honey, are you listening to--


          HUSBAND
I feel like an Arch Deluxe. Mm, and fries.
Supersize it!
```

72 The proper way to communicate that a character does not complete a thought is with an ellipse (. . .).

```
          WIFE
He never listens . . .
```

73 Ellipses (. . .) work best when used sparingly. If every character has an ellipse after the last word they speak, you run the risk of every character "sounding" alike on paper.

74 Use contractions as you script the dialogue so it reads as if spoken more naturally. *We have won!* vs. *We've won!*

Keep Slang Fresh

75 When giving characters a language of their own, you may find it valuable to create slang. Including the latest words or phrases from the urban and youth cultures can date your material, so it's better to be creative when putting words into your characters' mouths.

- *Buffy the Vampire Slayer* uses creative slang in the expression "What's the sitch?" (meaning, *What's the situation?*).
- In *Clueless,* the phrase "As if!" is used in response to, "Will you go out with me?" "As if!" (meaning, *No!*) is creative slang.

These phrases sound contemporary and fresh, and the meanings are clear.

76 Use colloquial words to create dialogue that sounds as if it's being spoken. Invest in a slang dictionary to see how these words look in print. Screenplays in which *yeah* is spelled *yea*, *yah*, or *ya* can make your work seem amateurish.

Give Your Characters a Code

77 The best way to underscore to a Hollywood Reader that characters have history is in the dialogue. These characters will communicate via verbal shorthand or vocabulary that they use only when together. The Hollywood Reader picks up on this immediately and you've come closer to creating a whole identity and realistic relationship.

For example, male coworkers will talk in code, using words from hunting or bowling to describe what took place off-hours in order to avoid creating a hostile environment in the office. Through code, the two can carry on a private conversation by the watercooler and passersby have no idea of what they're talking about. But the reader (and the audience) knows what's being said.

Convey an Accent Without Losing the Hollywood Reader

78 Keep in mind that this is not the 1890s, so writing *do, dem, dat* to convey an African-American talking is offensive.

79 Dialogue that changes the spelling of words to communicate an accent (*vee tink vee haf eet*) may be indecipherable and distracting to some Hollywood Readers. It's usually enough to say that a character speaks with an accent, then reinforce their origin through sentence structure. Compare *Vee* *go der now* with *We go now.* The *We go now* conveys that this character hasn't mastered the finer points of English grammar while still managing to communicate what he means.

80 An exception to the above tip is when a character speaks garbled nonsense. Make this obvious by the responses of the other characters.

When to Use Repetition in Dialogue

81 Repeat information in dialogue only when you want to dramatize the character's changing point of view or a character flaw. If in one scene Carly tells police that the other children on the playground were taken by aliens, then relates the same incident in another scene but claims that three women took the children, you communicate more than the abduction—you reveal that Carly isn't telling the truth or doesn't know the truth. Repeating information without showing something about your characters wastes space and slows your story's momentum.

Dialogue and Action

82 Interweaving action with dialogue gives scripts a cinematic feel by adding movement and interest to a scene. Doing this also adds authenticity because people rarely engage in a single activity.

> MOLLY
> Any man who saves my life and reads "Green
> Eggs and Ham" over the phone at 2 a.m.? I
> want a committed relationship with that guy
> because--

```
Suddenly, QUICKSAND sucks Molly down . . .

                    MAX
            Close your mouth! Breathe through your nose!

Molly nods as she sinks.

MAX GRABS HER HAIR

and pulls her up up up . . .
```

The more you integrate action with dialogue, the more you communicate a sense of reality unfolding on the page.

83 Dialogue that explains what the visuals and action cannot is the most effective, interesting, and efficient dialogue.

84 Eliminate dialogue that narrates the action. If Jim watches Baker win a footrace, there is no need for Jim to say *Baker just won the race!* to the spectator next to him.

85 Similarly, eliminate dialogue that states the obvious. If your two police detectives see that the thug they're chasing is in a glass elevator headed for an upper level, showing the elevator ascending and one detective saying to another *Up there!* is redundant.

86 In action sequences, dialogue seems most realistic when it takes into account what the character is doing with his or her body. Even the most verbose character will speak in brief phrases or single words when running for his or her life.

87 Wherever possible, eliminate questions requiring a *yes* or *no* answer. These stop the dialogue and often the answers are too easy for the reader to anticipate. Replace the questions with open-ended questions that expose more of your characters' thought processes, personality, originality.

88 Focusing on one subject for too long can slow your story's pace. More than two or three pages of dialogue in which characters wrestle with the same issue without making a decision or introducing new information can force the Hollywood Reader into skimming.

89 While you want the dialogue to move your story forward, too much of a good thing can overwhelm your audience. Monitor the flow of information through your characters scene by scene, taking care not to send out more information than can be absorbed in a single setting. The Hollywood Reader should be able to pick up the one, two, or three points in each scene. Barrage a Hollywood Reader with too much information at once (especially in the opening act) and she may not absorb the information and become confused later in the screenplay because she missed an important point. Ditto for the audience that sees your movie in a theater and can't rewind to figure out what just happened.

90 Each dialogue exchange should spark a reaction from the other characters. If your characters go through the motions of communicating without hurting, comforting, informing, or somehow impacting each other, it suggests that your story lacks tension and impetus and the scene lacks a point.

Make each encounter between your characters count for the story.

91 Dialogue that serves as a discovery process for your characters will fascinate most Hollywood Readers. Don't be afraid to show your characters in process as they learn the truth about themselves, others, and circumstances.

Dialogue and Backstory

92 When you include backstory in the dialogue, keep the information brief. Small phrases like *We met at Riker's in the '50s* sprinkled through the dialogue go a long way toward revealing necessary backstory. But always make certain that the backstory you include is absolutely necessary for us to understand your story and characters. If it's not, excise it.

Silence

93 What your characters choose not to say is as important as what they do choose to say. Consider your characters' silences in conversations as seriously as you would consider their words.

Misunderstandings

94 Nothing reads as more authentic than characters who misunderstand and misinterpret each other. If you find your characters communicating with 100 percent effectiveness to each other, rethink your dialogue. Supereffective communication robs you of wonderful opportunities for conflict and comedy.

The Right Fit

95 If you come up with a great line of dialogue, save it for a scene where the fit is exquisite, even if it means filing the line away for use in a future screenplay. Beautiful lines tossed into marginal scenes stand out as misfits.

Finally

96 Let your characters speak for themselves. While an occasional screen direction indicating how a character should deliver a line can be helpful, using this kind of direction throughout the screenplay can distract the Hollywood Reader and undercut the dialogue's power to speak for itself.

Style That Turns On a Hollywood Reader

★ ★

Your writing style *can be an asset or a liability to the story you tell. Either the style enhances and brings to life the story and characters, or it gets in the way of these elements.*

Because good screenwriting is minimalist in terms of the details you want to include in a screenplay, it's important to explore the style that ace writers employ. There's a reason for the lean, economical style popular today: It works. Not only do the pros convey the essence of what happens on the screen in a few well-chosen words, but they do so in a way that captures the attitude of the moment.

Your goal in writing a screenplay is to create an all-encompassing experience for the Hollywood Reader, the same experience that the director and stars involved in the project will have to pick up on when they translate the elements to the screen.

*You're not writing to please a reader—you're writing to com-
municate a total experience that translates to the screen.*

The Inside Scoop About Style

An experienced Hollywood Reader can tell from the writing
on the first few pages of a script whether or not the screenwriter has the craft down pat. These tips show you how to get
it right.

Style Tips

97 Write in the present tense to convey that the action is
unfolding in front of the Hollywood Reader's eyes. For example, *Lexy chases Aaron into the lake* has more energy and immediacy than *Lexy has chased Aaron into the lake* or *Lexy will
be chasing Aaron into the lake.* Your goal is to have the action
unfold in the present as it unfolds on the page.

98 Writing in word pictures can close the gap between
what you envision and what you communicate to the Hollywood Reader. Compare *John, a short, stocky, strong-looking
man* with *John, a fireplug of a man.* Strive to be vivid, succinct,
precise in your descriptions.

99 Describe only what is necessary for the telling of the
story. Characters' thoughts, backstory, and hopes are not com-
municated to the audience unless you put them into the dialogue or action. While it may be a credit to your character
development that Randy bears a tiny facial scar from a fight

with now dead Tommy, there's no point in describing it unless the scar impacts Randy's personality, appearance, or the story.

Clarity

100 Write in a way that makes your meaning absolutely clear. *The father of the bride, who is running this year's Boston Marathon* is ambiguous. Compare with *The bride, whose father is running this year's Boston Marathon*. The less ambiguity, the better.

101 Take care to choose only those words that convey your *exact* meaning. *Aaron flops into the water* communicates a different attitude about Aaron's skill and motivation in the Hollywood Reader's mind than *Aaron leaps into the water*. Each word carries weight.

102 Know the meaning of the words you use and know how to use the words in context. *Seven-month-old Stevie was so titillated when his three-year-old brother rubbed the feather against his cheek that he laughed out loud*. The word *titillated* is not used correctly. While it means "tickled," it has erotic connotations. Be careful to use words whose meanings and connotations you understand completely, or you risk the Hollywood Reader questioning your meaning and losing track of your story's flow.

Lean Out

103 Excise extraneous words so that your writing is lean. Economy of language is a strength in screenwriting. Compare these two descriptions:

- *A luscious flamingo-pink Victorian with lacy white trim around the windows and porches, the porches cluttered with a crisscross of wicker lawn furniture that is all curls and cushions*
- *A pristine pink Victorian*

A screenplay often conveys the *essence* of what will happen on the screen, not the precise details, so fewer words are needed to communicate the action. If you really want to go for it when describing a scene or two, pick your battles. A screenplay provides only so much space to tell a story. If you've got an important setting, do it up but don't skimp on scenes, dialogue, or action.

Scripting Action

An action screen story has to generate excitement as scripted or it's going to be a tough sell.

104 Make sure the action flows with logic.
- *Randy JUMPS from one building to the next, then slides down the side of the second building.* Because ordinary humans cannot slide down vertical structures, the action is illogical. If your character has a special ability, tell us about it beforehand or make it stand out, as done in this next example.
- *Randy JUMPS from one building to the next, then SLIDES (!!!) down the side of the second building!*

105 Use ALL CAPS when scripting pivotal moves in action sequences. This way even the least experienced or most careless Hollywood Reader will notice the important moves and elements (the bomb, the baby, the bullet). The moves and elements will also stand out to those involved in the production later on as props are organized and a shooting schedule is readied.

- *Molly uses the moment to THROW HERSELF at the Second Man—pushing him OFF THE GONDOLA to his death, screaming all the way down!*
- *BULLETS riddle the roof.*

106 Maintain a conversational tone when scripting action sequences. *The car lurches. Joanie laughs. Oops.* This streamlined writing style can pull in the Hollywood Reader and keep her involved in your characters' action. Note how the conversational tone communicates a mood in addition to detailing the main beats of the action.

107 Emphasize verbs to make action sequences exciting. Compare *The car lurches. Joanie laughs. Oops* with *The car skids wildly and stops suddenly. Joanie giggles her shrill, silly, nervous laugh.* Verbs keep the action moving, adjectives almost always stall the action. Also notice that when you have more words, you risk diluting the reader's impression of the action. Action conveyed in a few words moves faster on the page than action struggling under the weight of too many modifiers.

108 Breaking blocks of action description into paragraphs of between one and three lines of type can make the action read more quickly and ensure that the Hollywood Reader will not miss important moments. When paragraphs detailing action run from six lines to a half page, these almost always communicate that the screenwriter has included too much minor information about character movements and that the action is overly detailed. The goal is to communicate the *essence* of what the actors will portray on the screen. Ultimately, the director decides on the details of the action's choreography.

109 Similarly, break long sentences or important moments of action into phrases to minimize the possibility of the Hollywood Reader misconstruing your meaning. If breathing is what you want to emphasize in a scene, write *Inhale. Exhale.* Each thought or moment of action can be its own sentence.

Punctuation

110 Convey excitement, build suspense, and show drama with the way you script the action sequences. Using exclamation points, italics, and underlining to highlight surprising movements can help express the excitement of the action you envision. *Junie leaps headfirst into the cake and <u>DISAPPEARS</u>! LaCrosse investigates, nose to the frosting.*

111 While the use of underlining, italics, or boldface for highlighting pivotal or unusual movements can help your work have maximum impact, save these tools for moments that really count. Overuse can dilute their effect and even cause the reader's eye to move down the page, skimming only those underlined or italicized words or phrases. Write in a way that forces the reader to read every word.

112 Avoid semicolons when scripting action and description. Semicolons are awkward and risk stopping the

Hollywood Reader's eye in scene description and action sequences. Compare the following descriptions:

- *Jim gets out of the police cruiser; scopes out the street; approaches the closed-off hostage situation.*
- *Jim gets out of the police cruiser. Scopes out the street. Approaches the closed-off hostage situation.*

The second example reads faster than the example using the semicolons, and that's the goal of a screenplay: to create on paper the sense of immediacy that you want captured on the screen. That's how the pros write. Staccato. Economical. Not always proper English but always the best way to convey the mood and the action happening in the imagination.

Make Your Story Move

113 Get right into the scene's action after the slugline when possible.

```
EXT. COLORADO RIVER WHITEWATER -- DAY


Waves assault Dana's raft. A monster wave pulls her
UP, flips her OVER, slams her DOWN.
```

114 Take a pass through your script, weeding out unnecessary adjectives and paring sentences down to only those words essential to the communication of your thoughts. The result will be a higher-caliber script.

115 Delete camera angles and other technical descriptions unless you are also a director. These can detract from the project, especially if you have limited experience and aren't making the best choice of shots. Better to use your screenplay to do the writer's job: developing characters, dialogue, and a story.

Jennifer Lerch

Editorializations

116 Consider editorializations or asides to the Hollywood Reader as smart-bombs: Use one or two per screenplay and save them for driving home a point like nothing else can.

> *Jack and Tina kiss. (Remember what happened the last time they kissed? It's happening again . . .)*

When you talk during the script, you take your Hollywood Reader out of the movie. It's like talking during a movie. Shhh!!! Show, don't talk. Excessive use of asides slows your story's momentum, detracts from your characters and plot, and even causes the Hollywood Reader to forget the flow of your story.

117 While a few well-placed asides to the Hollywood Reader can jazz up a screenplay, phrases like *The best action scene ever!* or *The biggest explosion in cinematic history!* indicate the reverse is probably true. It's best to let your story and characters speak for themselves.

The Tone

118 Always treat the Hollywood Reader like an insider when explaining intricate details or technical terms. Taking a patronizing tone (*For your information, dear Reader,* which I have actually seen in a screenplay!) can be offensive and risks alienating the only ally you may have. Also worth remembering: Once the script analyst recommends your screenplay, the next Hollywood Reader is the executive's assistant or the executive! If you take a patronizing tone with him or her, you risk losing the support of the person you're trying to win.

119 Writing that communicates with kindness, humor, and a sense of "We're all in this together!" marks top screenplays.

English Not Your Native Tongue?

120 Have a firm grasp of the English language if submitting a screenplay written in English. If English is not your native tongue and if you are unfamiliar with the nuances of the language and contemporary American culture, consider working with a partner who is strong in this area. Awkward writing can get in the way of even the best story and characters.

Creating a Concept and Characters That Will Sell Your Script

These next chapters explore the concept and the characters, two elements that, if done well, can make your script stand out in the reader's coverage report.

How does it work?

The average Hollywood Reader's coverage report goes straight to the desk of the Story Department head, who reviews it and then sends it on to the Executive Reader (who can work for a talent agency, a studio, a network, or a production company). The Executive Reader is a little bit different than the Hollywood Reader in that the stakes are higher for him or her. This Executive Reader wants something to sell out loud in a conversation—in a pitch over the phone or in a face-to-face meeting. The essence of your story and characters has got to be summed up in a few catchy words or phrases. It should look good on a one-sheet or in a *TV Guide* ad. It needs to smack of obvious appeal because the executive's job rides on the ability to choose projects that will ultimately pay for themselves. Stories that don't have some kind of hook to grab audiences (and the Executive Reader) will probably not interest enough moviegoers to make a return on the initial investment.

Creating a concept that sells itself and characters who spring to life in the opening lines of a reader's coverage are what you want to shoot for. These sections show you how to do this in a way the Hollywood Reader will appreciate.

20 Tips on Creating a Concept That Sells Itself

✶ ✶

From the minute the reader opens your screenplay, she's trying to answer these questions: What's it about? What's the concept? How do I sell this to my boss?

As you answer some of the same questions when developing your screenplay, check your concept against these tips to make your project sell from page 1 of the reader's coverage. A concept that can be summed up in a catchy phrase or two is more likely to sell than a concept that takes several sentences to describe. Strive to isolate the essence of your story and gauge its commercial appeal before you send out your script to the Hollywood Reader.

High Concept

121 *High concept* is how readers refer to those stories that have a catchy idea and broad appeal. A *high-concept* screenplay can be sold without lengthy explanation by the Hollywood Reader or the Executive Reader. In *Liar Liar, a lawyer <u>has</u> to tell the truth for 24 hours.*

Issue-Oriented Concepts

122 Create a concept around an issue we can root for passionately. Choose a concept that translates into a story interesting enough to tell. If it doesn't sound good coming out of your mouth, it's probably not going to be a successful pitch.

123 In issue-oriented screenplays, always personalize the issue around which you build a concept. A concept detailing the horrors of toxic waste has more impact if narrowed to one mother's fight against toxic polluters after her daughter is permanently crippled as a result of illegal toxic dumping.

Elements Found in Most Salable Concepts

124 Build into your concept a hero/heroine whose weakness makes achieving the goal difficult. An illiterate mother fighting the toxic polluters who crippled her daughter has more of an uphill battle than a mother who is a top lawyer.

125 Build a concept around a conflict and characters audiences can root for. A dog that savagely kills its owners and then embarks on a search for new owners is a tough sell unless you're telling a horror story. However, a dog that loses its human family and then embarks on a search to be reunited with them is going to be easier to sell, especially if the canine overcomes great obstacles along the way. (Remember *The Incredible Journey?*)

126 Grow your concept out of a conflict that compels the Hollywood Reader to learn more about how the conflict is resolved and keeps her turning your script's pages quickly.
A woman sells her baby to survive, then has second thoughts and undertakes a daring rescue mission that could cost her life.

127 Create a concept that taps into a profound human experience like love, loss, revenge, or coming of age. The more universal your characters' problems, the more likely the Hollywood Reader can relate to these on a distinctly personal, gut level.

128 Keep your concept logical.

After years of trying to prove her intellectual supremacy against a much older genius, a four-year-old [think about it] wins the title of World's Smartest Person.

A concept can cut its own throat with inconsistencies like these.

129 Show in the concept that the outcome is important. This suggests that you have a story worth telling. *Hubert the spy's daughter Eliza slowly kills herself with drugs.* That's sad but not compelling. Compare it with *Eliza's addiction compels her to sell out her spy father and compromise national security.* Now, *that* captures attention. It's instantly more important when one person's self-destruction affects innocents.

Give Your Concept a Good Hook to Grab the Hollywood Reader's Interest

130 Hook the Hollywood Reader's interest by playing into a familiar circumstance that takes a bizarre or ironic turn. *The Twilight Zone* made a series out of storylines that hooked us in with quirks like having a man return home from work only to find that his house and family are gone and nobody ever remembers them existing.

131 Play into a human fantasy. *Warren wins the lottery . . .* One of the tests of successful entertainment is whether or not it provides fantasy fulfillment. Not all entertainment can accomplish this, but you've got something worth developing if you create a concept with this promise.

Having a Tough Time Coming Up with Something New?

132 Create a uniquely challenged lead character to solve a tried-and-true conflict. This can capture the notice of top acting talent.

A blind woman holds pillaging Nazis at bay for a week before the Allies arrive, saving her town.

133 Tweak a cliché concept by adding a unique setting.

An astronomer saves the world from alien invasion in the Middle Ages.

134 Put an unexpected lead in a role usually played by an expert.

A bookish librarian is forced to impersonate a leader in the sex slave trade so the feds can rescue newly kidnapped victims.

Genre Hybrids

135 Capture reader interest by crossing wires of genres to create something utterly unique. Think about creating something like the werewolf/western, or aliens meet caveman (*Stargate* meets *Quest for Fire*). The idea is to crossbreed genres to create a new genre that captures interest and announces itself as something original.

136 Update a classic. Take *Robinson Crusoe* and deconstruct this classic into a contemporary love story so the reader doesn't realize she's dealing with the timeless story until she meets the girl named Friday and the guy named Crusoe trapped together on a desert island. Or use the Orpheus myth as your source and expand on that. Set the myth in space, and have Orpheus beam down to a planet to find the woman he loves, then bring her back.

137 Reinvent familiar heroes in new genres. Remake Albert Camus's *The Stranger* as a cop thriller, set *Swiss Family Robinson* in space, or whatever else your imagination can construct.

138 Some unique conflicts defy classification. (Remember *Forrest Gump*?) If you've come up with one, go with it.

Think Commercial—It's Not Crass, It's Just Good Business

139 When crafting a concept, think ahead and imagine what the poster of your movie would look like. The question execs often ask is, *What's the one-sheet look like?* The studio exec asks this so he knows how to sell his boss on your idea. It's a pitch, but sometimes a concept *is* a pitch.

Think You Have a Great Concept?

140 Summarize your concept on paper to ensure that it has a hook, implied conflicts, and an outcome the Hollywood Reader will care about. If your concept lacks one of these ingredients, keep wrestling until you create a concept that sells itself.

Characters the Hollywood Reader Recommends to Top Stars

★ ★

In the words of one Hollywood agent, "Think not what the star can do for your script, but what your script can do for the star."

Your script has to be more than a vehicle that puts a star before an audience. It should provide an opportunity for the star to express something new as an artist, to participate in an amazing story, to be part of one of the best projects to come out of the industry.

Top readers at talent agencies know this. From the moment these readers encounter the characters in your script, they're trying to visualize them, know them, guess what they'll do next, and see if this character could be the next one to win that client an Oscar.

Readers everywhere want *to like your characters and to identify with them for other reasons, as well—they will experience life through these characters in the next 120 pages, much like the people who pay $$ to see your screen story in a multiplex will do.*

Authentic, original characters can get the industry's power players interested in your screen story and can take even a standard genre piece to another level.

Bottom line: No matter what kind of script you're writing, it's to your advantage to feature characters who breathe with life. These tips show you how.

10 Most Common Flaws and How to Fix Them

141 *Clichés.* Be a cliché buster. Clean house in your script by giving the hooker with the heart of gold a deceitful streak.

Assign your Donna Reed–like mom a raging temper or a mean streak. Give a hard-drinking, world-weary, divorced, middle-aged police detective a positive outlook on life and a dream to retire to Paris, France. Clichés garner words like *predictable* and *stereotypic* in coverage—judgments that can be avoided with a little creativity.

142 *Do-nothing characters.* Delete low-energy characters from your script. Not every character needs to act as though they're on speed, but you do want characters to pursue their dreams with vigor and single-mindedness. If Sonia wants drugs, keep her searching for them. If a subplot has detective Manny wanting to grow award-winning tulips, have him pursuing this dream at every turn. Hold reader interest by keeping your characters busy and deeply involved in their interests.

143 *Indecisive characters.* Eliminate most indecisive characters from your script. Scripting characters who make decisions and carry through with action is a key to keeping your story moving forward. Characters need not be rash, but if your story involves Twyla's pursuit of a dance scholarship, we need to see Twyla going after the scholarship with everything she's got for the story to hold interest.

144 *Passive characters.* Turn your passive characters into proactive characters who make things happen instead of letting the action happen to them. Nobody wants to root for a wimp.

145 *Too-sudden transformation.* Make the act of change an extremely difficult process for your characters to undergo.

A character who is frightened to leave the house in one scene, then just closes her eyes, steps outside the front door, and realizes she loves being in the crowded street may seem like a ridiculous example, but this kind of sudden, too-good-to-be-true change is common in marginal screen stories.

146 *Characters who are too good to be true.* Remove goody-goodies from your script. Every character worth recommending is a mix of positive and negative traits.

147 *One-note characters* who are always content, angry, disturbed—you get the idea. Characters need to hit more than one emotion, express more than a single thought throughout the story if they're to seem multidimensional to the reader.

148 *Lack of believable motivation.* Provide your characters with sympathetic motivations the Hollywood Reader can understand and root for. If John wants to be a cosmetic surgeon because they make lots of money, we're not going to root for him through tough days in medical school. If John wants to be a cosmetic surgeon to repair the faces of children with birth defects, we're going to find it easier to stay interested in his struggles, especially if he's got kids in his life who need the skills he's developing.

149 *Inconsistent motivation.* Decide what compels your characters into behaving the way they do and keep the motivation the same throughout the story. Inconsistent motivation not only makes your characters seem inauthentic or flighty, it also can make your story seem unfocused and arbitrary.

150 *Inconsistent characters.* If Oscar doesn't know anything about the bomb in one scene, then suddenly remembers seeing the bomb earlier, that's an inconsistency. If Tanner ignores his wife in one scene, then hangs on her every word in another scene, that's an inconsistency (unless you're showing a personality disorder).

10 Ways to Make Characters Spring to Life

151 *Give each character a distinct world view.* This world view should filter everything the character does and says. Howard believes the glass is half empty and is depressed at every turn, grabbing for whatever he can take because it's only going to get worse tomorrow. Blaze believes the glass is half full, is upbeat because life is only going to get better—there's plenty to go around, and he lives and gives freely because there's no chance of running out.

152 *Assign your characters idiosyncrasies* to imprint your characters on the Hollywood Reader's imagination. Does Jack pull on his ear, blink, or clasp and unclasp his hands when he gets upset? Details that appear with consistency throughout your script breathe life into your characters and can be used as cues to show what's happening inside the character. Actions do indeed speak louder than words in a screenplay.

153 *Develop your characters' backstories* to get the Hollywood Reader behind him or her, communicating where they've been and how their history plays into their present attitudes. You can do this as simply as by saying *George, three ex-wives haven't dampened his enthusiasm for marriage.* Newborns aside, every character should have had a life before the story opens.

154 *Integrate attitudes and values* toward things like food, trust, color, style, education, politics, religion, and more into your story. Even if your characters never engage in discussions of these particular things, their attitudes will be apparent in their conduct and decisions. Know your characters' interior landscapes and they will become a part of your story's exterior landscape in one way or another.

155 *Give your characters a home.* From a cardboard box in an alley to a Park Avenue apartment, communicating a character's domestic situation better enables a Hollywood Reader to visualize a whole person. We know where they sleep and how they live, and understand their values a little better because we've seen their home.

156 *Give each character a dark side.* It's worth repeating: Don't fall into the common trap of having your characters be Pollyanna-ish. Every character needs a dark side, an area of weakness that provides an "in" for unpleasantness or conflict in his life. Even the good guys in your story need some dark areas if they're going to come across as realistic.

157 *Every character needs a flaw,* a personal failing that he is not aware of. While a character may be conscious of his dark side, a flaw is usually a blind spot. For example, Larry thinks it's a mark of his virility that he keeps a parade of women revolving in and out of his life. He doesn't realize that his promiscuity grows out of deep insecurity and fear of commitment. Bozell thinks it's a mark of self-actualization that he gets what he wants from people. He doesn't realize that he's walking all over them and alienating everyone he bullies.

158 *Create resourceful, smart characters,* people who dig deep and use whatever they have to meet a challenge, and *then* run out of what they need. Their need at this point will seem much greater to the reader than a need that the character doesn't even try to meet himself.

159 *Characters who are not prepared for what happens keep the reader rooting for them.* A woman whose baby dies suddenly, an atheist who suddenly comes face-to-face with a God he does not believe exists, or a fashion model who loses her face in a car wreck will hold reader interest as she sees how the character handles this unexpected turn.

160 *A sense of humor makes any character more appealing* and realistic to a reader. The character need not actually be funny—the other characters in the story can roll their eyes at the lame jokes and observations—but there's something that smacks of reality as a character tries to keep the ups and downs of life in perspective through the use of humor, be it dry, wry, dark, or absurd.

Effective Transformation

161 The best characters have transformation at their core—it's this process of forcing a character into the painful process of change that draws top talent to roles and imprints certain characters onto the cultural imagination.

162 *Plot character growth.* As you plot your story, plot simultaneous points of character growth. If Sadie will ultimately walk away from her life of crime, show the critical points in her move from criminal to law-abider during the course of your story so that your screenplay has a sense of being integrated.

163 *Choose a struggle for which a reader can root.* A man who practices his marksmanship so he can kill Bambi just for the fun of it is going to be a tough transformation to root for unless your story is a dark comedy that includes social commentary. While a struggle need not be pretty or slick, it generally cannot be a struggle that the human psyche innately roots against or you face an uphill battle in generating reader interest.

164 *Provide an origin for the character's desire to change.* The desire to change must spring from something that happens during the story so the reader understands why the character wants to alter her way of living. This usually happens during the first act, when the character realizes that the way she operates no longer works. For example, criminal Sadie gets pregnant and wants to give up her criminal ways before the baby is born.

165 *To be realistic, character changes must be gradual and show signs of struggle.* Sadie will have to wrestle with resisting crime, and chances are she will probably cave in to her habitual criminal impulses a time or two after making her decision to go straight. Only gradually will Sadie endure experiences that will cause her to turn completely, irrevocably to a new life. But this turn will involve blood, sweat, and tears. If the change is too easy, it's not worth the paper it's scripted on. Readers want to root for tough things.

166 *Keep the outcome a mystery until the final act.* There's no telling what the outcome will be—will Sadie ultimately be able to walk away from crime, or will she give in one last time when the stakes are at their highest? You as the writer know where you're taking your character, but the audience doesn't know if Sadie can go straight, and we don't want her to have her baby in prison. The resulting tension from knowing the possible outcomes, knowing that our character stands to lose a great deal if she caves in one last time, creates suspense. And suspense holds reader interest.

5 Ways to Beat the Reader with Relationships

Staff Hollywood Readers at one legendary studio are directed to choose those screenplays that present the most interesting, authentic relationships. Decide that relationships between characters matter in your story, no matter what kind of story you craft—be it a romance, a mystery, or a supernatural thriller.

167 *Keep relationships mutually beneficial* to seem believable. If John gets nothing out of his friendship with Roger, their connection won't ring true. Characters must get something from the time they spend with each other, even if being with another person simply shields them from being alone. Decide what your characters are getting out of each relationship, even if the trade they make is a foolish one.

168 *Work out issues through each relationship.* Each relationship provides a natural context for working out issues in your screenplay. If Dave's only reason for driving in the squad car with Phil is so that there can be two good guys on hand to take on the two bad guys lurking in the dark alley up ahead, your story will seem unsophisticated, contrived, and one-note to the reader.

Use your characters' relationships to play with ideas, examine issues and themes, and generally add some weight to your story—even if the story is a piece of fluff. Even undemanding audiences recognize that fluff can be more satisfying if it explores issues like love, truth, the perils of stealing, and the like.

169 *Decide how your characters feel about the other characters in your story.* Does Marjory have a superiority complex? Does Harry resent his know-it-all older brother Mark? This is yet another way to turn your characters inside out for the reader, exposing their interior landscapes so that the personalities you create seem realistic and are ultimately unforgettable.

170 *Show the relationships between your characters* rather than detailing this in the description portion of the screenplay. It's stronger to show Marva and Tony fighting than to describe them as "an embattled couple." The reader knows that the audience who sees the screen version of your story cannot know that the couple is embattled unless you show this through action.

171 *Play character relationships for all they're worth,* using conflicting motives and old tensions between characters to complicate the story and move it forward. Sam's struggle with resentment toward Ezra causes him to hesitate before running into the burning building to rescue Ezra. In that moment of hesitation, the roof of the burning building collapses, and now Sam faces almost certain death if he dares embark on a rescue mission. Use the relationships to complicate your story, aggravate your characters, cause hurt or joy—you get the idea. Motivate the action through the relationships.

Sidestep Age-Related Flaws

172 *Keep your central character the same age for most of the story line.* This will allow the Hollywood Reader time to get to know the character, understand and identify with the conflicts, and establish consistent rooting interest.

Why? It's tough to root for a character whose age keeps changing, because in many ways a character is a different person at different ages. A five-year-old girl will be much different than a twenty-five-year-old version of herself (hopefully). Usually when you want to show a character at different ages, it's to make a single point (like, *The people in her life kept dying*). If this is the case, make your point quickly and then move on.

173 If your story requires that you show your lead character at different ages, make the scenes showing these ages *sig-*

nificant so the Hollywood Reader sees the connection to the rest of the story. Make your points with enough drama and punch that they stand out.

174 If you show your lead character at different ages, make the scenes doing this *brief* so they don't take up a disproportionate amount of your screenplay. Usually the scenes that bring the reader up to speed on a character's backstory by showing different important events in their life can be scripted in one fourth to one half a page. If you find yourself scripting scenes and sequences that go on for several pages, find a briefer way to make your points.

Beat the Reader with Character Age

175 In using characters to write a screenplay the Hollywood Reader will recommend, tailor-make a character for an actress in her 40s, 50s, 60s, 70s+. Even marginal screenplays offering proactive, interesting roles for this age group get consideration at talent agencies—the ladies we loved when they were in their 20s and 30s want to keep working and they have few roles from which to choose! Be the one to write that beloved star the role that will bring her back to the screen and win her an award in the process.

Create a Protagonist and Antagonist Who Will Start a Casting War

★ ★

Nailing the two key personalities in your screenplay can make or break the story. You can create a unique concept, but if you can't create a protagonist a reader roots for and an antagonist the reader roots against, chances are you're not going to be the writer whose screenplay takes that concept to the screen. In fact, that great concept may not even make it to the screen if you can't convince the reader that it can be pulled off in a story.

Don't let that happen. Treat your characters like royalty. Make your characters king no matter what your genre. Then make your protagonist and the antagonist the kings over all other kings.

Correcting 10 Common Protagonist Flaws

176 *A subordinate character is more interesting.* Make your protagonist the most interesting, appealing character in the story, because that's the character the Hollywood Reader spends the most time with. Flip the roles and create a story around the more interesting character if a supporting player *consistently* steals scenes from the lead.

177 *A protagonist without a flaw.* Your protagonist *cannot* be perfect if the reader is going to root for him. Every character needs flaws, but a protagonist especially needs some serious flaws that make his growth during the story a necessity if he is going to accomplish his goal. The course of the protagonist achieving the growth also provides your story with some wonderful opportunities for suspense. Will timid Gregory master swordplay enough to survive the final duel?

178 *An unappealing character.* A protagonist needs to have an element in his personality that attracts us if you hope to garner rooting interest. We root for the alcoholic in *Leaving Las Vegas* even though he is intent on drinking himself to death, because we sense his hurt and vulnerability.

179 *No clear goal.* Every protagonist needs a clearly delineated goal to inform the story and show the reader what to root for. Without a clearly defined goal, the protagonist is probably going to wander pointlessly from one scene to the next and your story won't build the momentum needed to carry it to a rousing climax.

180 *A silly goal.* We've said it before but we'll say it again: Give your protagonist a goal that shows he is smart and a goal for which the reader can root. Amanda wanting to count all the frogs in the world may be a cute goal for a quirky little girl, but it's not the kind of primary goal that will engage an audience.

181 *The pursuit of the goal is not impacted by the protagonist's weaknesses.* Relate your protagonist's weaknesses with his ability to achieve his goal. In *Liar Liar*, the lawyer learns how to function without lying, which is a major stretch because he lies constantly. Integrate the character's growth with the story's outcome, and you create a very strong way to sell a reader on your project.

182 *The protagonist changes his goal mid-story.* Keep your lead character's goal consistent. The circumstances may change, the goal may prove to be more difficult as the protagonist becomes engaged in the conflict, but if Barry sets out to save the girl, have him save the girl even if it means saving the world in the process. When your protagonist's goal shifts, your story needs to begin building momentum all over again. You also risk your story coming across as haphazard to the reader.

183 *The protagonist gets rescued.* Keep your protagonist self-sufficient. He can get help, but he needs to do the dirty work, discover the clues, and ultimately fight the battles himself for the story to satisfy. A strong protagonist has to be the only person who can resolve the conflict. If he's not the only one who can do this, why have we been rooting for him?

184 *An unconvincing protagonist.* Show why the protagonist is worth rooting for instead of detailing these reasons in the description. Show that Marta loves her baby by having her stay up all night rocking the sick infant. *Show* it, don't say it, if you hope to convey essential information to the audience in the screen version of your story.

185 *A protagonist who doesn't grow.* A protagonist who is the same person at the story's end as when the story opened is going to be a disappointment. This goes back to the transformation notes in the previous section (numbers 161–166). The growth of the character adds suspense to your story. Use it for all it's worth.

10 Tips to a More Effective Antagonist

186 *Make your antagonist equally strong (or stronger) than the protagonist.* What makes the story of David and Goliath worth telling is that a normal-sized teen defeats an adult warrior giant. A milquetoast villain means your protagonist controls the situation and too easily finds a way out of his predicament, weakening a Hollywood Reader's take on your story.

187 *Introduce the antagonist early in the story, even if he remains only partially disclosed.* The reader needs to know that the antagonist is an organic part of your story and not a last-minute addition.

188 *Provide concrete reasons to root against the antagonist.* Show the antagonist's handiwork. If Sam wants to get ahead at work, show coworker Dave stealing Sam's ideas, spreading lies about him, attributing nasty e-mails to him. We can't root until we know what we're up against.

189 *Show what's at stake if the antagonist succeeds.* Clarify what will happen if the dragon is allowed to live, the pirates continue unopposed, the little girl cannot fight against her tormentors.

190 *Create a complex antagonist.* An antagonist who exudes pure evil from page 1 works in some stories, but most stories need an antagonist to be a blend of light and dark, with a gradual revelation that what once appeared to be light is actually dark. For example, Fred shelters alleged killer Sharla, who is on the run from authorities. Sharla eventually learns Fred is the real killer. That makes Fred more dangerous than he would have been because he is a skilled liar on top of being a killer.

191 *The less cartoon-like you make your antagonist, the more rooting interest your screenplay generates.* A flat, all-powerful, all-knowing, all-wicked personality limits your story. Put some humanity into your antagonist to show the tragedy of what he has become. This can give your story a note of tragedy.

192 *Keep your antagonist strong.* An antagonist with an obvious weakness or suddenly revealed area of vulnerability can provide a too-easy way for your protagonist to defeat him, thus weakening your whole story. Think *Terminator* and *Die Hard*. A strong antagonist challenges your protagonist into working hard to complete himself and conquer his weakness so he can defeat the antagonist with this new self-knowledge and strength in Act 3. A strong antagonist almost ensures a suspenseful story and exciting climax.

193 *Keep your antagonist's powers, talents, and resources within the realm of the plausible* (at least in the universe of your story) in order to keep him believable. Nobody can be and do all things.

194 *Keep your antagonist's powers, talents, and resources consistent throughout your story.* If the Joker suddenly begins flying like Superman, we begin questioning your story's plausibility. Create your antagonist and keep him consistent.

195 *Make your antagonist reprehensible, even if this is only apparent in hindsight.* Even if this antagonist appears to do something kind at one point in the story, clarify later on that he acted out of self-interest in this instance of apparent do-gooding. If the reader doesn't want to root against the antagonist, you undermine the rooting interest of your protagonist.

Create Effective Nonstandard Antagonists

The Antagonist That Is a Group

196 *Personalize your antagonist if you choose to make it a group.* If your protagonist fights a group, give the group a leader. The best stories have faces to go with the forces animating them.

> *While explorer Buddy fights an entire tribal nation, it is the nation's lead warrior who spearheads the assault against Buddy. It is this person Buddy must dispose of if he is to survive.*

197 *Identify in descending order the most dangerous members of that group.* A mob head can have dangerous bodyguards and hit-persons at his or her disposal. Your story will be stronger if you give faces to all the most lethal persons your protagonist faces.

The Antagonist That Is a Force

198 If your antagonist is a force (like the wind, the sea, the winter), *keep that force a consistent part of the story* if it is to seem real to contemporary audiences. If Kurt tries to survive winter while lost in the Rocky Mountains, keep the weather growing in ferocity as the story progresses. As the temperature drops and snow falls, Kurt's struggles to survive will intensify as he faces an increasingly hostile environment.

199 Just as when battling a more personal antagonist, *the protagonist often needs to refer to the force as he or she would refer to a personality.* You can accomplish this by having your protagonist refer to this force as a person and directly addressing it. While this may read as the person talking to himself, the scenes can be very powerful as the protagonist personalizes this impersonal force through direct address.

Part 2

* * *

Acts 1–3:

Writing for the

All-Important

Audience of One

Certain things must take place at different points in your screenplay or the Hollywood Reader, like the audience who may eventually see your screen story at the multiplex, may come away from the experience feeling dissatisfied. While no two screenplays are alike and while each genre and story may need to adapt screenwriting principles and theories differently, it's smart to accomplish some basic goals no matter what story you write.

Page numbers are tossed around as we talk about the different parts of a screenplay. These form a rough guide. Within basic parameters, there are no hard-and-fast rules in terms of scripting the length of a screenplay the reader will recommend. The only time a reader will pay attention to the number of pages is when first seeing the script (*Is it fat?*) and when the story slows. The latter parallels the moviegoing experience. The only time a moviegoer looks at his watch is when something in the story isn't working and he suddenly finds himself outside the experience and thinking about other things. Ditto for the Hollywood Reader who suddenly becomes aware of page numbers when something isn't happening in the story.

Act 1 Goals

The typical Hollywood Reader expects the first part of your screenplay to hook her fast and not let go. As you dangle that hook in front of the reader, she's going to expect to meet your main character, understand his situation, get an idea of his goal, and see what he faces as he attempts to go after that goal. And you're going to want to do this in about twenty to thirty pages. Usually stories that don't accomplish these goals in this amount of space are moving too slowly, but it's rare that a script can do more than this in twenty to thirty pages.

These first pages of your screenplay also tip off the Hollywood Reader to whether or not you've got a commercial concept, can develop colorful characters, and understand the basics of screenwriting.

Goals to Achieve in This First Act

* *

200 Establish the story's genre (comedy, mystery, horror, romance, etc.).

201 Hook the Hollywood Reader by creating a situation so compelling or a character so interesting that the Hollywood Reader genuinely wants to find out what happens next.

202 Introduce your story's protagonist. This protagonist is your story's main character. He (or she) appears in most of the scenes and will resolve the central conflict.

203 Commit your protagonist to a course of action so the reader knows who she's rooting for. For example, the protagonist will risk his life to rescue the baby or to save the world from aliens.

204 Create and introduce your story's antagonist (the person, force, or group that opposes your protagonist).

205 Commit your antagonist to a goal and a course of action that are diametrically opposed to your protagonist's goal and course of action. Often (but not always) your reader knows that she is rooting against this person, or at least what this person stands for.

206 Create and introduce the central conflict (the problem that the protagonist struggles against throughout the story).

207 Set up your story's subplots.

208 Introduce your story's secondary and supporting characters.

209 In terms of writing the first act of a feature-length screenplay, you should shoot to be between 20 and 30 pages into a 100- to 120-page screenplay by the time you complete this act.

Setting Up Your Story for Success in Act 1

★ ★

Your script's setup can literally make or break your project in the Hollywood Reader's eyes, particularly at some companies that instruct readers to stop at page thirty of a script if it looks substandard. You may have a great second act and climactic sequence, but Hollywood will never see it unless you give it a savvy setup.

7 Common Flaws in the Setup

210 *Absence of an appealing character.* A salable setup has an instantly appealing character who elicits sympathy through his circumstance. The Hollywood Reader needs to know who to follow in the action, who to root for, who the story is going to be about, who to invest her emotions in. Without this knowledge, the reader is drowning in the sea of events and people you flood her with.

211 *An illogical or disjoint sequence of events.* The sequence of events that establishes the setup must have a flow of reason that makes sense. The events must all add up, even if you create a fantastical story. If Herman plants a beanstalk, then leaves town on a business trip and eventually moves to Tahiti because he likes Polynesian women, the setup (planting the beanstalk) makes no sense because it bears no relation to the events that come later. However, if Herman plants a beanstalk, climbs it, learns about the world of giants and uses this knowledge to impact his own world, the setup has a logical progression as events build a consistent story.

212 *The setup is flat—it doesn't intrigue, beg questions, leave us wanting more.* The effective setup presents a situation that begs further exploration—we want to know *What happens next?* If Olympian Tawnee is diagnosed with a degenerative disease and decides to compete in one more Olympic Games in spite of her health, we want to see how she manages to face other athletes while simultaneously battling an inner nemesis.

213 *The setup seems disorganized and doesn't build to a point.* A good setup is often organized into two sequences or groups of scenes. These sequences build toward the story's big idea. The first sequence develops the character's situation. The second sequence develops the character's strategy for dealing with the situation and provides the premise for the rest of the story.

- *As she recovers from the emotional effects of a rape, public defender Lucy takes the serial rapist case.*
- *After battling peer pressure to use drugs, thirteen-year-old Dylan shoots up for the first time.*

In each of these examples, the part of the sentence that comes before the comma provides the first sequence. The part of the sentence that appears after the comma provides the second sequence. The whole sentence summarizes the entire setup.

214 *Characters seem like an accessory to the action as events happen to them.* An effective setup forces the character into making a big decision—a decision that focuses and gives impetus to the rest of the story. A character needs to take the upper hand and challenge events if the setup will interest us in him. Lucy may be recovering from the psychological effects of rape, but she's determined to move through the hurt as she throws herself into a case that forces her to face her painful issues.

215 *No show of cause and effect between the events and the characters.* The reader must be able to see the effect the events are having on the character to understand the decision the character will make toward the end of Act 1. That's the way to get the reader behind your characters during the rest of the story.

216 *The setup goes on and on—it doesn't know when to stop, it has no sense of pace.* While a reader isn't going to look at page numbers when a script works, a setup that goes on indefinitely draws the reader's eye to those numbers.

A rule of thumb: Each of the two sequences in a good setup usually runs between ten and fifteen pages and contains several scenes that build to a specific point. If straitlaced Sylvia is going to commit a crime during the story, use the first ten to fifteen pages developing Sylvia's straitlaced personality, then invest the next ten to fifteen pages developing a sequence that shows Sylvia deciding to commit the crime. Using this general page guide can help you pace your story. If your setup is too complicated and is running too long, you may be trying to cram too many events into the setup. The reader looks for two major climactic moments in the setup, no more.

217 Know the difference between a setup and a story. The *setup* is the initial situation or series of situations that start your story and spring your lead character on his quest. The *story* includes the setup, complications, and an ultimate resolution to your character's problem. A clever setup isn't enough to get a Hollywood Reader's recommendation—a good story is. *Holly swears off men until she meets Tom* is a setup. What Holly does after meeting Tom provides the story.

218 The amount of material you include in your story's setup is as important as the material you leave out of it. Avoid attempting to cram an entire story into your setup. One clue that can help you decide if you are attempting too much: If your characters travel great geographic or emotional distances during the setup, you are probably forcing too much information into too few pages.

3 Tips for Testing Your Story's Setup

219 Answering these questions about your setup can provide a quick test of whether or not it's doing the job in your story.

- Do the events in the setup change life as your characters know it?
- Does your character make a decision that irrevocably changes the story's direction and his life direction?

Be brutally honest as you answer these questions. If your setup is illogical, awkward, or disjointed, you jeopardize the rest of your story.

If your setup makes sense, you pull the Hollywood Reader

into your story, get her rooting for your characters, and are on your way to getting the positive coverage often needed to sell your screenplay to decision-making executives.

220 Summarize your story's setup on paper so you can see the relationship between the two elements of the setup. If you cannot summarize your setup in a single sentence, refine it until it makes sense on paper. You'll save yourself hundreds of hours of time later in the story and in rewrites if you get your story off to a solid start. You also can see how the Hollywood Reader will summarize your setup.

221 Answer three questions others will ask about your script if it moves up the Hollywood ladder:
- Would you buy a script with this setup if you were a studio executive?
- Would you want to play the lead role if you were a top star?
- Would you pay for a movie ticket to see the story unfold on the screen?

If you answered "no" to any of these questions, rework the setup so that you are able to answer "yes."

Grab the Hollywood Reader with Your Opening Sequence and Don't Let Her Look Back

★ ★

First impressions endure. Start your screenplay off strong and show the Hollywood Reader you can craft an exciting, alluring, intense experience. The goal is for the opening sequence to grab the Hollywood Reader and not let her go. You want her invested in your story, rooting for your characters, turning the script's pages as fast as she can. You want her to shut the door, to forget about lunch, and to recommend your script as soon as she reads FADE OUT.

A good opening sequence is a great way to get your career rolling. A sluggish or bland opening sequence puts you in an uphill battle in terms of winning over the Hollywood Reader. Don't settle for second best. Get it right from page 1 rather than have to work extra hard later in the screenplay to make up ground.

Page Count

222 The opening sequence in a professional feature screenplay often runs between ten and fifteen pages in length and contains between three and five scenes. An opening sequence that runs longer cues the reader that you don't understand structure and pacing and/or don't know where your story is going or what it's about. While a reader may not be looking at page numbers, she knows about how many scenes it takes to build up to something. If the opening takes too long, she knows she's in for a long, slow ride.

The Content of the Opening Sequence

223 The reader looks for two things in an opening sequence: the introduction of your protagonist and the revelation of his or her situation.

- *A rent-a-cop gets suspended for maiming a shoplifter.*
- *An advice columnist gets dumped by her boyfriend, whose unsigned letter she answered in a negative way.*

You've got to put some substance into the sequence if it's going to impact the reader who experiences it.

224 The opening sequence sets up the next ten- to fifteen-page sequence, which will introduce the script's premise. If your opening sequence does something other than this, rework it. The reader has her mouth open and is ready to swallow the hook—if she could only find it. Hook your reader! She wants to get into your story!

When to Open Your Story

225 *Have a good reason for opening your story when you do.* Examine your options: Would the story be more dramatic if you opened it before or after Lucinda delivers her baby, before or after the baby is kidnapped from the hospital nursery? The reader will consider the way the opening sequence plays into the rest of the story and the relationship it has with it. Explore your options before the reader explores the options in her coverage. Make the opening sequence work hard for the rest of the story.

In Doubt About When in the Narrative to Open Your Story?

226 *Open later rather than sooner.* Most screenplays take too long to get into the conflict that matters to the rest of the story. If your story explores sheltered Iowa farm girl Monica's experiences after moving to New York City, your goal is to get Monica to New York City as soon as possible so we can share her experiences there. Showing thirty pages of Monica wondering if she should move, making the decision, saying good-bye to family and friends, and driving away is waiting too long to get us to the setting where the story (her experiences) takes place. If, however, your story is about those events that lead Monica to leave Iowa, then the bulk of your story should be set in Iowa. Nail down the specifics of what your story is about, then get your character into the place where the conflicts erupt as close as possible to the opening scene. That's the way to show the reader that you understand what your story is about.

227 *Open your story as close as possible to the introduction of the central conflict.* This way you ensure that your story focuses only on the most interesting, relevant events. When a Hollywood Reader wades through dozens of pages of setup, the screenplay is a tough sell to the executive (who will not do any wading).

Using the previous example, if the story explores Monica's experiences in New York City, she should run into difficulty in New York City as close as possible to page 1, and at least by page 15. If you wait longer than this to give Monica a significant problem, you risk losing the Hollywood Reader.

In Your Script's First Scenes

228 *Foreshadow where your story is going in the opening sequence.* The first thing you show your Hollywood Reader is what she is most likely to remember and it sets up the rest of your story.

- If your story explores voyeurs, have someone watching someone else.
- If your story is about aliens, show the sky, something falling from the sky, build a sense of wonder that anything can happen, or some like thing to create a mood and set up your story.

Even if your story thrives on randomness, take care in choosing the images and use them to build the experience you story conveys.

229 Overly detailed montage opening sequences scream *Skim me!*

Why? The opening sequences you've seen in movies as the titles play are filmed at the director's discretion—they aren't so detailed in the screenplay. The pros know this, the amateurs don't.

To indicate a montage, briefly describe the series of shots and short scenes. For example, a shopping spree, a string of assassinations, preparation for a wedding. Then get on with your story.

Conflict in the Opening Sequence

230 *The sooner conflict erupts, the sooner you hook the reader.* Establish your character's conflict in the screenplay's first scenes, if possible. If not, bring on the conflict ASAP to hook the reader (and eventually the audience).

231 *Introduce your central conflict in the opening sequence if possible.* The closer to the opening you place this important scene, the sooner you communicate your story's direction to the Hollywood Reader. Experience teaches that many (although not all) of the best scripts start fast. Write to win the reader from page 1.

Keep the Opening Sequence Fast Paced

232 Reconsider skipping ahead days, months, or years in several of the opening scenes as you setup your story. Covering too much time can undercut your story's impact because it chops up the story line and doesn't allow enough time for conflicts to brew and momentum to accrue. It also doesn't help the reader focus on what your story is about and where it's going, information that an executive reader doesn't have the time to wait until page 18 to find out.

Characters in the Opening Sequence

233 We said it before and we'll say it again: Introduce the protagonist as soon as possible so the Hollywood Reader knows who to root for, gets to know that character, and makes an emotional investment in him. When you get the reader rooting for your people, you've got that reader eating out of your hand. And that's where you want the Hollywood Reader at all times.

234 Make the entrance of significant characters memorable to get the reader's attention and cue her into the fact that this is SOMEBODY. The reader doesn't have the cues that movie audiences later will have (the movie poster, the star in the lead role, the movie previews).

> *JENNY arrives, all stilettos and sequins, flashes her FBI badge, and leaves the POLICE CHIEF in a cloud of perfume.*

235 Show your characters fighting back so the reader sees that you've created proactive personalities who aren't going to take it lying down—characters we can root for throughout the story line. Have kidnap victim Roger fight against his captors even if he is risking death. Nobody wants to root for a wimp unless that wimp is going to transform into an aggressive survivor during the course of the story.

236 Show your characters' personalities in the opening sequence so the reader gets a vivid idea of who she's dealing with in terms of their life, their talents, their job, who they are in the world. Give your character something to do that expresses who he or she is on the inside.

237 A tip-off to rare craftsmanship: Connecting the lives of your characters in the opening scenes. The sooner the lives of your characters intertwine in your story, the more organic the story will come across. Organic stories, those which seem completely integrated, are often recommended because of their fine craftsmanship. As you make each element connect with the story's other elements, you eliminate the sense of randomness that lower-level projects consistently rely on for cohesion.

Opening Sequence Flashbacks

238 If you show a climactic event (for instance, a suicide) in the story's opening sequence and then flash back in time during the rest of the screenplay to show what led up to that event, it's imperative that the story line contains some remarkable twists. Have a great reason for giving away your conclusion in the opening scene if you hope to engage the reader through the rest of the story line. It's the sense of mystery, of the utterly unexpected, that keeps a reader interested.

Avoid This Deadly Flaw

239 Don't spend the first fifteen pages of your screenplay explaining your character's backstory. If your character or the main situation has a complex history that cannot be boiled down to a few short scenes, begin your story earlier in time and feed the reader your character's history through the story structure, piece by piece, making it a part of your story's plot and not something that happened years ago. Plotting your character's growth as you plot your story makes your script come across as integrated and organic.

If at all possible, however, boil down the backstory to a few key scenes. For example, if you want to show why explorer Ned in the present day searches for treasure lost 100 years ago, write a brief opening scene(s) detailing a mutiny aboard a cargo ship containing the treasure. Show that the ship is captained by Ned's ancestor. Then move to the present, show Ned's group deciding to go for the treasure and heading off on their boat. The goal is to get the main characters off on their quest as quickly as possible with only the explanation needed to have their quest make sense.

Backstory is best handled in simple, to-the-point scenes that set up your main story in a minimum of pages.

Fulfilling the Reader's Expectations as You Open Your Genre

★ ★

Once a Hollywood Reader identifies the genre of your story, she brings certain expectations that you must fulfill in the opening sequence if your script is going to get recommended. Sound unfair? These are the same expectations studio heads, stars, and audiences have when dealing with genres.

Comedy

240 Create a funny opening sequence to pull the reader into your comedy and prove you write funny. You face an uphill battle convincing us that this is a project to recommend if your opening is flat.

Opening a Romance

241 Convince the Hollywood Reader that the protagonist will benefit from love in his life. Do this in the opening sequence and you have the Hollywood Reader rooting for your character to find *the one*.

242 Prove that your protagonist is lovable. Klutzy Marvin may be dumb, but he's got a warm way about him, an admirable devotion to his autistic brother, and the unsinkable belief that he's going to succeed in life. Characters need not be perfect, but the reader must see something appealing about your character to root for him or her.

Thriller

243 Hook the Hollywood Reader into caring about your lead character's welfare and you're one step closer to a reader recommendation. It's tough to root for the welfare of a despicable lead, and in fact you may get the reader rooting against your lead if you create too abhorrent a character.

244 In a thriller, build suspense right from the start and show that all is not well through the adjectives used to describe the setting, the action, and the characters. While a romantic comedy may open on a bright, sunny day, a thriller may open on dark, stormy night. As always in screenwriting, choose your adjectives with care and use them sparingly to make them stand out.

Horror

245 While the horror genre thrives on testing the human limits of enduring manifestations of the dark side of the universe, take care not to fall into the trap of creating stereotypic characters as you attempt to juxtapose the normal with the barbaric. Keep your characters realistic but unique, identifiable in their humanity on an emotional level but unique enough for the audience to enjoy and be entertained by them for the duration of your story.

Conflict: A Reader Can't Recommend a Screenplay That Doesn't Have It

★ ★

Conflict is the most important component of your screenplay. Without conflict your character has nothing to do, you have no story to tell, and the Hollywood Reader—how can she sell a screenplay that's not really about anything to an executive?

These tips can help you create or refine a conflict important and complex enough to sustain a feature-length screenplay, and interesting enough to hold the Hollywood Reader and the audience that may pay to see your screen story at the multiplex.

Correct the Most Common Conflict-Related Flaws

246 *Lack of conflict.* This is *the* most common reason this Hollywood Reader rejects screenplays. Adding plausible, exciting conflicts is one of the simplest ways to enhance any screenplay.

247 *The conflict is simplistic or superficial.* Make the conflict a difficult, complicated one for your character to resolve—one that takes time, planning, and a little bit of luck to achieve. This ensures that your story has room to grow and can go the 120-page distance.

248 *The conflict is made up, silly, or ridiculous.* The conflict must seem realistic on some level to grab a Hollywood Reader's rooting interest. An eighty-year-old woman taking on the Miss America Pageant and sacrificing everything to win clearance to compete will be a tough sell to a reader unless you find a way to make the goal more plausible (or unless you're scripting a comedy).

249 *It doesn't matter what happens.* Be sure the Hollywood Reader clearly understands *why* the conflict is serious, why the protagonist needs to achieve his goal (to save the world, win the battle, catch the criminal).

250 *There's nothing at stake.* Building on the previous tip, one way to show that the conflict matters is by showing what will happen if it is not addressed successfully. Not every genre can put a character's life at stake, but every genre *can* put something tangible and valuable at stake as your protagonist struggles with the central conflict. You generate legitimate tension from a Hollywood Reader's point of view when you risk the quality of life, treasured relationships, or well-being of your main character or those people that the main character loves.

251 *There's something at stake, but we don't care about it.* There is a relationship between rooting interest and the value of the thing at stake. A rule of thumb: The more primary the relationship jeopardized by the story's outcome, the more the Hollywood Reader will root for the desired outcome.

A parent saving his or her child will read as more compelling than an adult saving a prep school classmate he never liked.

252 *There is no relationship established between the protagonist resolving the conflict and simultaneously fulfilling his destiny.* Clearly show how achieving the goal will enable your protagonist to fulfill his destiny, becoming more of the person he (and we) sense he should be. Not only will daddy Rob save the baby's life if he retrieves the child from kidnapers, but he will have a chance to be the father that he was meant to be.

253 *The conflict is too narrow—the conflict affects only one person.* Create a conflict that involves other characters in your story. This increases rooting interest because it raises the stakes: If the protagonist doesn't come through, others suffer.

If widower dad doesn't learn to love again, he will never remarry and his young children will never have the mother they need.

254 *The conflict is a retread. We've seen it so many times before we know the story by heart.* Add a new twist to a stale conflict. Check back with the section on concepts (page 61) for effective ways to do this through creating a genre hybrid and more.

255 *The conflict is an odd fit with the lead character.* Create an organic relationship between the conflict and the lead. There has to be a reason why nobody else but your lead character can be the one to resolve the conflict.

Putting the Central Conflict in the Spotlight and Keeping It There

256 From the minute she reads the words FADE IN on page 1 of your screenplay, the reader is waiting for the central conflict to be unveiled. Don't make her wait longer than page 15. Sooner is better. If you place the conflict later in the script, you risk the reader assuming either you don't know how to pace your story or that you don't know what your story is about.

257 Make your story's central conflict the most compelling, juicy, interesting problem in your story so the reader keeps turning the script's pages to see how it's resolved.

258 Make your central conflict take up most of your characters' time, even if your characters have other interests. This proves to the reader that your characters are actively engaged in resolving a significant problem. Even James Bond spent more time resolving the central conflict than dallying with women.

259 Show how the central conflict relates to the protagonist as soon as possible. If detective Jenny is to solve the crime dramatized in the opening sequence, assign her the case in the first act. That's just one more way to prove to the reader that you understand what your story is about.

260 Define the protagonist's goal and situation early in the *dialogue* portion of your screenplay so the goal doesn't risk getting buried in the scene and action description. This ensures that the reader won't miss it, and neither will the audiences who later see your movie.

261 You can change the size or scope of the central conflict (and hence the protagonist's goal) in subsequent acts, but it's best not to narrow the conflict. The bigger the problem, the more intense the reader's rooting interest. Think big.

262 As you evaluate your central conflict, know that great conflicts explore universal themes and relationships. This kind of conflict can make even a flawed story resonate with enough truth so that it impacts the Hollywood Reader and gets further consideration.

263 In most genres, your character's *emotional* focus should be on the main problem facing him. Often this is most effectively accomplished by investing the protagonist heavily in the individual who is jeopardized.

Spy Celia falls in love with the double agent she's assigned to kill.

264 As you craft the central conflict for a character-driven relationship drama, keep in mind that the Hollywood Reader needs to see more than a story about a troubled person—she needs to see a story about a person in trouble.

Heide's claims of physical pain and mental anguish will seem like so much hot air unless we see the source and understand that her life and the life of her unborn child could be in jeopardy if intervention does not occur.

Give your characters legitimate problems, not problems that can be handled with a few counseling sessions or with a prescription of Prozac.

265 Create conflict at every turn. While most of us abhor conflict in our lives, when it comes to stories conflict between characters equals interest. Think of ways to pit your characters against each other. Be ruthless, be nasty, but get that conflict onto the page to wow the reader and intrigue audiences.

266 The more you can turn your characters who share the closest of relationships against each other, the more profound a sense of conflict you create. This is why a story of betrayal often works best if those betrayed are family members. We'd hate to experience what we're seeing on the screen. That's a great rule to write by.

Create Ongoing Conflict to Keep Your Story Rolling

267 Pile the problems onto your protagonist so he has enough to do during the story. If the car gets towed with

Nancy's baby in it, have Nancy chase the car, get stopped for a pedestrian infraction, get thrown in jail, then learn too late that the tow truck carrying her car has been stolen and is already in international waters as thieves ship it overseas.

It only has to be real in the universe of your story, not in the universe in which we live.

268 The best conflicts have events as well as people conspiring against your characters. Instead of a one-in-a-million lucky break happening to your character, make a one-in-a-million *unlucky* break happen.

Teen Wendy has sex for the first time and contracts HIV.

Subplots and Conflict

269 Nail down your story's primary, secondary, and tertiary conflicts and develop each with less screen time in descending order so you convey a well-organized story to the reader. More screen time devoted to less important conflicts dilutes your central conflict.

270 If you find that a subplot usurps your central conflict in terms of interest or excitement, consider making this subplot the central conflict and changing the focus of your story. It's rare that a screenplay gets recommended on the basis of a strong subplot, with the contingency that the main storyline be dumped.

271 Hollywood Readers love organic screenplays in which every character has a similar goal.

- In *Star Wars*, each of the major characters shares the same goal (to survive), even though each has his or her own personal agenda or reason for wanting to survive.
- In *Something About Mary*, everyone wants Mary (the detective, the old classmate, the pizza delivery guy).

Everybody *can* want the same thing, but they're going to go about getting it in a slightly different way and for slightly different reasons.

Following the Opening Sequence

272 Explore the questions (or conflicts) your story has introduced and find a way to address these questions in what follows in the forthcoming story. It's one thing to draw in a Hollywood Reader and quite another to deliver all that you promise.

273 Set up several layers of conflict in the first act to give your story different dimensions and intrigue a reader who may not be interested in the primary conflict but who may be intrigued by the secondary conflicts. (There's no accounting for taste!)

274 Connect the story's opening sequence clearly to the subsequent action so that the Hollywood Reader sees continuity. If you show a theft in the opening sequence, the theft should play a significant role in the rest of the story. Don't kick off your story with an unrelated gimmick.

Prevent Reader Whiplash: Handle Backstory with Care

★ ★

The details related to the events your characters experienced before the story opens are important for you as a writer to know but aren't always relevant to the story you tell in the screenplay. Deciding how much of a character's past comes into play in a story and integrating this past neatly into your screenplay can be tricky.

275 Poorly integrated backstory can put the brakes on even the most fast-paced story and take the reader right out of the movie experience you had going. Find a way to integrate backstory without interrupting your story's flow and while contributing to the mood, character development, and forward momentum. If Lisa falls in love with Ed, the process of her learning about his past can provide suspense, drama, or comedy, depending on your genre. The key is to make not only the information contained in the backstory work for your story, but to place it in the spot where it ups the ante for the character and advances the plot.

276 Communicate backstory as efficiently as possible through pieces of brief conversation, voice-over, or visual elements. Massage your concept further if your story cannot be told without significant backstory—i.e., if it takes pages and pages of information to communicate your setup. Your story's forward momentum can stall out when you put characters into reverse by probing the past in detail—unless, of course, exploring a person's past *is* your story. Vignettes can add color, but find a way to use backstory to keep your story in drive if you want to hold the reader.

277 Reveal backstory at opportune moments rather than every time you introduce a character. If your characters go into extended speeches about their personal history, or if other characters have to explain who so-and-so is and what they did way back when for that character to have meaning in your story, chances are you're doing more telling than showing in the screenplay.

278 When using a complex flashback structure, be sure that the information contained in the flashbacks moves your story forward and creates drama.

279 Avoid using dreams, flashbacks, and fantasies simply to spice up a stale tale. Most readers are as savvy as the audience your movie will play to—they've seen thousands of stories on television and in the movies. Use your imagination to come up with a new twist rather than a stale rehash. Imagination never goes unremarked upon in coverage.

Your Act 1 Checklist

★ ★

In this first act of your screenplay, you should have done the following to beat the Hollywood Reader:

☑ Established the story's genre (comedy, mystery, horror, romance, etc.).

☑ Hooked the Hollywood Reader by creating a situation so compelling or a character so interesting that the Hollywood Reader genuinely wants to find out what happens next.

☑ Introduced your story's protagonist. This protagonist is your story's main character. He (or she) appears in most of the scenes and will resolve the central conflict.

☑ Committed your protagonist to a course of action so the reader knows who she's rooting for. For example, the protagonist will risk his life to rescue the baby or to save the world from aliens.

☑ Created and introduced your story's antagonist (the person, force, or group that opposes your protagonist).

☑ Committed your antagonist to a goal and a course of action that are diametrically opposed to your protagonist's goal and course of action. Often (but not always) your reader knows that she is rooting against this person or at least what this person stands for.

☑ Created and introduced the central conflict (the problem that the protagonist struggles against throughout the story).

☑ Set up your story's subplots.

☑ Introduced your story's secondary and supporting characters.

☑ In terms of writing the first act of a feature-length screenplay, you should be between 20 and 30 pages into a 100- to 120-page screenplay. Remember: Page numbers are more or less arbitrary and should be considered a general guide for use in pacing your story.

Act 2 Goals

These are some of the things a typical reader may look for to-
ward the middle of your script (the second act):

Goals to Achieve in This Second Act

★ ★

280 A broadening of your story's conflict. Show that
the problem facing the protagonist is more far-reaching than
originally supposed so that the stakes are higher and the
reader has more reason than before to continue turning the
pages.

281 Serious complications in your protagonist's life so
that he runs out of his own resources and must gain new experiences, change his behavior, or learn a new way of operating
in order to resolve the conflict. Without major complications,
the reader has no reason to stay interested in the story because
there's nothing to root for.

282 Continued development of several subplots simultaneously with the main story line—otherwise, your story risks
come across as thin and one-dimensional.

283 Introduction of all subplots and secondary characters who have not yet appeared. Act 3 is too late to introduce new characters who will play an important role in your story.

284 Give your script the ultimate test to beat the Hollywood Reader: Synopsize the story in the same way that the reader will synopsize it in her coverage. Take several pages to tell your story—that's how readers at many studios and production companies present stories to executives. Write out your story in the same way that you would explain a movie to someone outside a movie theater. Hit the main beats, surprises, reversals, points of no return, the climax, and the resolution. Leave out none of the elements essential to the action.

285 Looking at your script's synopsized story, can you identify at least four main sequences in the second act? If not, you probably don't have enough activity happening. If your police story doesn't have about eight second act sequences, your story is thin, your screenwriting style is probably too loose, and you're probably not going to beat the Hollywood Reader until you take out the filler and toss more juicy conflicts into the mix.

Structure Tips to Help You Scale the Mt. Everest of Your Script

★ ★

Writers call the middle of a script Mt. Everest, Death Valley, the Grand Canyon. Readers call it Act 2. We all know it as the arguably most difficult part of the screenplay—the pages during which writers experience frustration and many readers yawn, count the pages until the script ends, and take a break to return phone calls.

How can you keep the reader not only reading your script but rooting for your characters and wholly absorbed in your story between pages 20 and 90?

Structure, structure, structure.

The Right Structure

Structure refers to the way in which you tell your story. It refers to the pacing, the order of events, how you ultimately put the pieces of your story together on paper.

Good structure, no matter which structure theory you subscribe to (and there are many in today's Hollywood), keeps the story unfolding rapidly enough to hold the reader's attention and keeps her rooting for the characters. Make sure your script's structure accomplishes these things for your story.

The Main Goals of Structure

286 Good Act 2 structure keeps the story moving forward so the reader has a reason to stay interested.
- If Tina searches for the elusive Blue Diamond, keep her on the trail and make that trail increasingly hot.
- If reporter Seth is on the story, show him investigating even though romance and health problems interfere.

Every element in the second act should be geared toward moving the story forward.

287 An engaging second act is paced so that it gradually builds tensions between the characters, tensions that will come to a head in the third act.

288 An engaging second act releases tantalizing information that enables your characters to piece together the motive for the murders, the identity of the killer, and the next logical place the killer will strike.

289 A second act builds the momentum that ushers us into the ultimate face-off that is the climax.

You can accomplish these four goals by breaking your script into sequences.

Sequences

290 Break down Act 2 into sequences. It will feel less like Mt. Everest and more like a hill you *can* climb. Manageable sequences will also unfold your story in steps so that the reader senses an organized, logical progression as the story develops.

How Many Sequences?

291 Most top scripts have from four to eight sequences in the second act. Each sequence is made up of from three to five scenes and should run about ten to fifteen pages in length. Of course, if your script has eight sequences, each sequence will be shorter than a script featuring four sequences and vice versa.

Sequence Structure

292 Each sequence should play like a miniature story in which the character establishes a goal, embarks on a quest, faces opposition which he overcomes, then is forced into creating a new goal. Structure each sequence with a beginning, a middle, and an end. The first scene in your sequence sets up the action. Complicate the action in the next two or three scenes.

293 Offer some resolution in the final scene of the sequence. While you don't want a tidy package that ties up loose ends and keeps your character comfortable, you do want the character to have gained knowledge about his situation or opponent during the sequence if the sequence is going to seem like more than filler.

Sequence Length

294 Every sequence has its own length. Let the sequence play out instead of keeping it uniform with the other sequences in terms of length. Why? If every sequence has the same length, your story will have a predictable rhythm that the reader and your eventual audience picks up on. Predictability is not good in screenwriting. The reader isn't looking at page numbers but will notice if something has a too-perfect proportion.

Slowing Down an Action Story Without Stalling

295 Even wall-to-wall action can be too much of a good thing sometimes. The way to vary the rhythm in an action story without stalling out or not meeting the demands of the genre is to create a scene that allows your reader (and your character) to catch her breath. For example, after a wild chase sequence, give your lead character a nice romantic dinner scene. While you don't want to hit a wall in terms of pace, you do want the scene to have a different feel than the chase sequence. Sidle up with this couple in a warm ski chalet, then follow this intimate scene with the baddies appearing outside the window waiting to burst in on the couple. Here we go again with more action as we head into a new sequence, but now we're ready to run.

Bridge Scenes

296 Connect your sequences with what one popular Hollywood executive calls *bridge scenes*—those scenes that connect two sequences. The romantic dinner scene used in the previous tip is a bridge scene. A bridge scene bridges sequences, allowing for a change of pace as you set up your next sequence.

297 Like all devices, bridge scenes are most effective when not used all the time. If you have sequence-bridge-sequence-bridge-sequence-bridge-sequence, you lull the reader into being able to predict what's coming up. And that's not the way to keep the reader (or your audience) on the edge of her seat.

298 A bridge scene can stand alone or be part of a subplot. Its function is to break up the action while moving your story forward.

Every Sequence

299 Every sequence should move the plot further along so the reader picks up on a sense of momentum. A sequence that doesn't do this stalls your story and gives the reader the sense that she's stuck in Death Valley.

300 Every sequence should advance the characters' arc to keep the characters growing and changing to meet the ultimate challenge that lies ahead in Act 3, at the climax. Without degrees of growth during Act 2, your characters' change will not ring true to the reader in Act 3.

301 Every sequence should include further development of your subplots.

Bang the Gong as Your Character Grows

302 To communicate character growth in a way that the reader (and ultimately the audience) will recognize, think of this growth as a gong. Every ten to fifteen pages (in every sequence), you want to bang the gong. This character note (the gong) will weave into your story a sense that the character is consistently growing. For example, as we plot a kleptomaniac's growth, we give him several chances to steal, and we show him stealing with ease and without remorse. Each time he steals, we're banging the gong. But then something happens as a result of a remark someone makes or as a result of a close call that convinces our klepto that he needs to change (another bang on the gong). He steals again, but this time it's tougher (gong). Gradually he stops stealing, he can't believe he can't steal, then he starts *returning* stolen goods (gong, gong, gong).

The key is to hit the gong often enough so that this element is a consistent part of the piece and doesn't read like a last-minute addition.

303 For greater suspense and to keep this gong from becoming predictable, keep our kleptomaniac's ability to overcome his problem under your hat—that adds suspense to your story.

Ending the Sequence

304 One of the best ways to end the final scene of a sequence is a reversal. During the sequence the character may take three steps forward and then experience a setback because of an unexpected twist or encounter. It's this piece of information that sets back the character which leads us into the next sequence.

```
Darryl limps through a mountain pass toward the cas-
tle to claim his rightful inheritance. He outwits
highway robbers, taking one robber's horse to ride.
Once down the road and safely away from the robbers,
Darryl learns the horse has magic powers--and a mind
of its own! Darryl fights the horse, tries to dismount
but cannot. The horse turns away from the castle,
sprouts wings, and drags Darryl up up up into the sky
and away from the castle!
```

Darryl ends the sequence having overcome an obstacle (the robbers) and arrived closer to his goal (the castle), but has another obstacle to overcome (a flying horse with a mind of its own). And the reader has a new reason to continue turning the pages.

305 However you end your sequence, the idea is to make these sequences seamless as they interconnect so that the reader is unaware of the story structure and sees the story as a unit. You do want some breathing room between sequences, but the key idea is to have the story unfold smoothly.

306 To prevent the sequences from coming across as un-related episodes, be sure that each sequence addresses the central conflict and continues building toward your story's climax.

Keep the Sequence End a Surprise

307 If Act 2 can be described as the Grand Canyon, consider each sequence to be the equivalent of whitewater rafting down the Colorado River. The boat might flip, the character doesn't know how to swim, may lose his life preserver, may become separated from the guide—may die! But you, the writer, know he's going to survive. Don't let on that the character won't die—only you know this, because when it comes to writing the screenplay, you get to play God. Relish the role and play it for all it's worth.

308 As you create sequences, use your imagination to come up with some ingenious twists. Lack of imagination causes the story to be predictable. Most readers have seen thousands of stories (haven't you on television, in the movies, and in books?). Most of us usually know what's going to happen next. Be the writer that shows the reader she doesn't know it all. Use your imagination.

Correct Common Act 2 Flaws

309 *Other characters hijack interest.* Take back your protagonist's story, put the protagonist in legitimate jeopardy, and feature the protagonist in the majority of scenes. This keeps your story focused and underscores to the Hollywood Reader that you know who your story is about.

310 *Other conflicts hijack interest.* Keep the central conflict center stage. Your main character's struggle should remain the biggest, most interesting concern in the story. Don't let a minor character struggle with something bigger and more interesting than your main character.

> *As two lead detectives investigate a serial murder case, a desk sergeant overdoses on Viagra and becomes a superlover to nursing home residents.*

Unless the Viagra sex incidents are part of the serial killer story line, edit them out. One set of incidents is comedic, the other set is serious, and you've got some sibling rivalry happening between story lines that are vying for attention.

Tips to Keep Subplots Working Hard for Your Story

★ ★

311 Pepper throughout Act 2 the subplots you set up in Act 1. These subplots should be consistent threads running through the fabric of your story. A rule of thumb: Try to interweave a subplot into each sequence so that you keep it alive in the reader's mind. You don't want the reader thinking, *Who are these guys again?*

312 Create subplots that develop stories you want to tell, not subplots that add an element that you think your script needs to sell. While your central conflict should be the most arresting conflict in the story, your subplots should be interesting, affecting, and entertaining in their own right.

313 Choose subplots that explore dimensions of the main story line. No good screenplay is a one-layer story. A real story has different dimensions as the protagonist's life comes apart and is put back together. The Academy Award–winning screenplay *Good Will Hunting* presents a simple, character-driven drama that has the title character struggling with loyalty to his friends, dealing with a romantic relationship, his therapist, the math mentor, and wondering about leaving the nest (Boston) and making his own home elsewhere. The conflicts converge on a single character, but through these subplots the story has different layers.

314 Each subplot should have its own beginning, middle, and end to seem like more than "filler." A subplot should be well thought out, a drama in its own right.

315 Complicate your story's subplots in this act so that they don't seem like afterthoughts to the reader. In Act 3, you will want to pay off these subplots.

316 Subplots can provide a great opportunity to hit your main character's gong, especially if the subplot is relationship oriented and provides an opportunity for your character to grow emotionally or in some other internal way.

Integrate Subplots

317 A good subplot always turns out to be related to and affected by the "A" story line. The two can be separate, but it's best to have the two story lines converge at some point so the reader sees a connection. If you want the man whose mother is dying in the hospital to have a romance with a nurse, interrelate the two story lines but always give the son/dying mom story line more screen time. The nurse can recommend medical treatments or receive secrets that the dying woman wants to get off her chest, secrets which impact the nurse's thoughts about her new boyfriend—your imagination is the limit. But find a way to integrate the plotlines so that they impact and interrelate to each other. That way the reader sees an organic connection and perceives that you've created a *story* and not just a series of random incidents connected by two strong brads.

318 If you can't find a way to satisfyingly integrate two plotlines that develop independently and don't intersect until the third act, rethink your story and eliminate one of the plotlines rather than have your script risk playing as fragmented and arbitrary. If Donald and May don't meet until the third act, if their lives and actions never impact or intersect before Act 3, chances are you're telling two separate stories. Best have each story line star in its own screenplay rather than forcing them into the same screenplay.

How to Avoid the Second Act Story Stall

★ ★

If you've followed the tips to this point, you've done a good job of kicking off your screenplay. You've got the attention of the Hollywood Reader. She's looking at your screenplay as a contender.

The next step is to keep your story interesting. No need to let Death Valley intimidate you. These tips can keep your story unfolding with excitement and intensity, no matter what the genre.

Tell a Good Story

319 The second act should present a story good enough to stand alone. The first act sets up this story, the third act

Jennifer Lerch

resolves tensions, but it's the second act that takes us to Oz. In fact, Oz *is* pretty much the second act in *The Wizard of Oz*. Make your Act 2 as adventurous and imaginative as possible.

320 Beware of the filler material trap: Don't use the second act as a bridge connecting Acts 1 and 3. Act 2 needs to generate its own excitement to hold the interest of the reader. Some readers expect the second act to provide a stand-alone story.

Raising the Stakes in Act 2

321 Exposing the evil the antagonist has perpetrated can give your protagonist new impetus to achieve the goal.

As detective Scott investigates nurse Lisa in relation to the mysterious deaths of infants in the hospital nursery, he learns that she's left a trail of dead babies in other hospitals during her previous employment.

322 Bring the consequences of the protagonist's failure closer to home.

When detective Scott realizes that nurse Lisa leaves a wake of dead babies in whatever hospital nursery she works in, he realizes that his wife has been admitted to the hospital and given birth, and their newborn is under Lisa's care!

323 As each sequence ends, worsen the potential for disaster (or misery, depending on your genre) if the protagonist fails to achieve his goal. This keeps the stakes escalating and the reader engaged.

The bomb is not only capable of taking out the building in which it's planted—it's found to be big enough to take out the entire downtown area!

324 There are instances in which a time limitation like a ticking bomb, a ransom that needs to be delivered to kidnappers within a set time frame, and other time devices can add suspense as the characters struggle to meet them. But these devices are overused and risk coming across as gimmicky if they don't fit your story. When deciding on what elements to include in your script, always be true to your story to tell a story that will ring true to your audience.

325 Consider using character opposition and reversals to sustain interest in the second act. If Jane and Betty kidnap Lulu, then Jane turns on Betty and suddenly makes a pact with Lulu, this turns the direction of the story and creates a whole new conflict that has onetime insider Betty on the outside. Like the warnings that come on other devices, use these only when they fit into your story. And of course, use them sparingly in your script so the reader doesn't begin expecting them every other page.

Conflict

326 Keep your story's conflicts significant. Make changes if the conflicts seem weaker and less threatening than in your first act. The key is to keep the conflicts fresh and compelling to the reader.

327 Keep the antagonist nipping at the heels of your protagonist to maintain tension and prove that he/she/it is a difficult opponent. A good antagonist never stays out of the protagonist's life for more than a few scenes.

328 Making the consequences for the protagonist's failure visual and physical in Act 2 can further enhance rooting interest. The building blows up, the divorce is finalized and the family splinters, the disease progresses and a loved one loses a limb—these are the kinds of visual consequences that can convince a Hollywood Reader the story will translate well to film.

329 Keep your characters' relationships in a state of transition to maintain interest. Have people go from being best friends to being rivals, from being happily married to outwardly combative, from trusting to distrusting. People don't go through events without having those events impact their relationships for better or for worse. Show your characters struggling to absorb the impact of the stress they're experiencing as they endure conflicts on all fronts in their world.

Keep the Pace Brisk

330 To keep your script's pace fast, avoid filler. Filler consists of the scenes you write to get to the scenes you *want* to write. Filler scenes are those scenes you don't care about. If you don't care about the scene, why will your audience (the Hollywood Reader) care about it? Filler is fat you can do without. Cut it.

331 Make each scene count like a move in a chess game. If the scene doesn't move the story forward, delete it.

332 Don't always telegraph what your characters are going to do. Show them in the scene doing it. Scenes that set up scenes can often be classified as fat. The leaner the script, the more the Hollywood Reader appreciates it.

333 Give characters a path for action as their problems build. If Sam's family is murdered, quickly put Sam on the trail of the killers. If Sam mopes after the murders, your story stalls. Keep your characters energetic and on the move so we stay interested in them, are convinced of their earnestness as they attempt to resolve the conflict, and can enjoy a fast-paced story.

334 Eliminate scenes in which characters rehash what happened in previous scenes unless this dialogue offers another point of view, a chance for comedy and character development, or new information that complicates the conflict. If you show Mr. Burns being found dead in his house, there should be a compelling reason to create five or six scenes in which characters tell each other Mr. Burns is dead. Otherwise, we only need one scene to tell us that he is dead.

335 Similarly, eliminate scenes in which characters talk about doing something, then do it in the scenes that follow. Amateurs do that, and amateur scripts generally drag in terms of pace.

If thieves map out an elaborate heist and then carry out the heist, that's a redundancy you want to eliminate. Know the difference between setting up scenes and giving away the action. Regarding the heist: Briefly show the characters casing the joint and otherwise making brief preparations, or just show the heist. The latter is stronger because it allows the Hollywood Reader to watch the action as it happens. It's a surprise. And readers love to be surprised.

336 For the sake of economy and organization, edit scenes that make the same point into a single scene.

337 Get in and out of scenes efficiently. If the scene gets hung up on obvious dialogue or extended description, cut the unnecessary verbiage.

338 Keep dreams, flashbacks, and fantasy sequences brief so the Hollywood Reader can keep track of what your main story is about.

339 Delete scenes that don't show new sides to your characters. One hundred to 120 pages doesn't give you enough space to waste spinning your wheels. Make every word and every scene count.

You Don't Have to Fall into These Act 2 Genre Traps

★ ★

Some genres seem to have Act 2 pitfalls that many writers stumble into, handicapping their stories. These tips address the most common problems related to genres.

340 The name of the game is to keep action moving, keep it surprising, keep it exciting. You do this through the use of set pieces.

341 Include several set pieces throughout Act 2 to keep the action moving and the excitement high. A set piece is an action sequence with a beginning, a middle, and an end. The set piece in a jungle could involve a stranded hero escaping from quicksand, saving a mute woman from pygmy cannibals, flagging down a cruise ship, beating off crocodiles, getting on board the ship and then discovering it's a ghost ship. The whole jungle experience is a set piece. The next set piece would take place on the ghost ship.

342 Spread the action evenly throughout the second act. Saving all your action for a single climactic set piece in Act 3 will be a tough sell to action fans who pay to see action and to the Hollywood Reader who cannot recommend scripts that don't deliver what the genre implies.

343 Provide a new wrinkle in the plot through the action. Action needs to work harder for the story than taking your characters from here to there—it needs to take the story into a new direction or to raise the stakes in Act 2.

344 Make the action in your screenplay original in terms of choreography. Show something different than the usual car chases, crashes, and bomb blasts in Act 2.

345 Do something unexpected with your characters as they travel in vehicles. It's often the integration of humor and personality into the action that marks the best examples of the genre.

346 Show a new aspect of a previously developed character in the action sequence. Use the fast pace and adrenaline rush your characters experience as an opportunity to give us new information about who they are, where they've been, and what they fear. Don't waste a great moment when everyone's paying extra-close attention to what's happening with the character by not disclosing something special in Act 2.

347 Keep the pace consistently fast in the set pieces. Don't allow your characters involved in a high-speed chase to suddenly have difficulty opening the car door as they attempt to engage the drug dealers in a foot chase. That slows the pace. The idea is to give the Hollywood Reader as big a rush as your characters experience.

348 Keep your characters from hiding behind gadgets. If you spend more time detailing the techno-gizmos in your screenplay than developing the characters, make some changes.

Romance

349 Conflict builds more chemistry between the characters in a romance than wrestling between the sheets in Act 2.

350 If you create an interloper who comes between two lovers, make that interloper appealing so that the attracted party experiences a real struggle about who to choose. The struggle is the conflict, and if the conflict is too easy to resolve you risk two things: making the character who must choose seem dumb if they can't make the right decision, and making the story too obvious.

Suspense

351 Resist the urge to build an elaborate plotline that reads more like a puzzle than a story. Place your characters at the center of your suspense story to ensure rooting interest.

352 The best suspense stories put an appealing character in jeopardy. The stronger a connection you build between the information and the character the Hollywood Reader cares about, the more impact your story makes.

353 Keep Act 2 of a suspense story interesting by having the Hollywood Reader work with the protagonist to solve the mystery. *Rear Window* does this beautifully as we watch the events unfold through the eyes of the character played by Jimmy Stewart. We identify so closely with the lead that when he is in danger, terror results.

354 Keep the knowledge of the protagonist even with that of the Hollywood Reader. Giving the protagonist information you withhold from the Hollywood Reader comes across as cheating.

355 Similarly, it flattens your story to tell the Hollywood Reader everything that's happened then make her wait while the protagonist bumbles his way into the same knowledge. Evaluate how the story's events are motivating the reader to stay tuned in.

356 To keep a suspense or mystery story interesting in the second act, introduce numerous interesting suspects who could have committed the crime. You handicap your plot with just one or two legitimate suspects unless you go into great detail and pit the two characters against each other, generating suspense in that way.

357 Plot reversals are key to maintaining momentum in a mystery or suspense story. Finding ways to show that the person we thought was guilty is actually innocent can take your story into a new direction and keep the Hollywood Reader turning the screenplay's pages.

Stay One Step Ahead of the Reader with Your Act 2 Story

★ ★

Keeping the reader guessing is the name of the game in Act 2. Because scripts are read first, staying ahead of the reader is staying ahead of the audience. An audience-friendly movie is a reader-friendly script.

358 Complicate, complicate, complicate the life and situation of your lead character. Lay on the obstacles thickly. Make it impossible for your hero to succeed, to achieve the goal. But always know that you will make a way to have that hero ultimately triumph. Keep your reader guessing, and your audience will also be guessing.

359 Learn to enjoy playing God. Unless you base your story on true life, the world you create within your screenplay is *yours!* You play with the information, exposition, character, and plot. Have fun.

360 Use red herrings, phony leads, false clues, and roads that go nowhere to win over the Hollywood Reader. A reader likes nothing better than to say, "Fooled me!" You can steer the audience and reader down a dark alley or into a forest— *you* control what they'll encounter there.

361 Give the clues about character and plot to the Hollywood Reader piecemeal. The name of the game is slow reveal, piece by piece. Hook 'em, tease 'em, tantalize, engage, then slow it down. A good script has a rhythm where you can push and pull, trick the audience into thinking the story or character is going one way and will do one thing, then have the whole thing go another way. A reader calls it a great script, audiences call it a great movie.

362 The way to engage the reader in Act 2 is to throw emotional as well as physical obstacles at your characters. If your antagonist enters a physical fight with the protagonist, think of an internal battle the protagonist fights as well. In this encounter, the protagonist fights the antagonist physically but himself psychologically.

363 Another way to engage in Act 2 is to get a sense that your protagonist is struggling and growing. He suffers a reversal, a defeat, a setback that makes achieving his goal unlikely unless he develops new skills and overcomes previously exposed weaknesses.

```
A football player loses his foot in a drunken acci-
dent that gets him kicked off the team. His replace-
ment foot, however, creates a second career as a
field goal kicker for another team, a ragtag bunch of
losers from the NFL. He has to beat his alcoholism,
deal with a phantom foot that itches, make it back
onto a team, and he's never kicked a field goal in
his life. But he wants to get back onto an NFL team,
and now he's got his chance. . . .
```

Keep a Good Thing Going

364 End Act 2 strong. A strong ending involves your character hitting rock bottom. Up to the end of Act 2, story has built toward a point of no return where everything is lost for the character and the story. This point of no return sets up Act 3. You want the reader to keep turning those pages to find out what happens to the hero. Without an *all is lost* scenario, the reader has no impetus to continue on.

Superman II provides an example of an *all is lost* scenario when Clark Kent trades in all of his powers so he can be with Lois Lane. He goes to the Fortress of Solitude, just a man, feeling powerless and facing the prospect that his planet will be destroyed. It's over—or so he thinks. That's how this movie ends Act 2. Clark Kent has made his decision . . . then he finds a little piece of Kryptonite, and that allows him to be Superman again. That's the redemption he needs—no sooner does he get his powers back than the story sets up the Act 3 confrontation in which Superman confronts the trio of baddies. Act 3 is all about being Superman again.

Finish Act 2 with your character in a slump and facing the end so that in Act 3 he can face a new beginning. It's a great way to jolt a reader into paying attention to the last part of your screenplay.

Avoid Common Flaws That Show Up in Act 2

★ ★

These are the flaws that often take the reader out of the dramatic experience you've been building and cause her to question your story and characters.

Carefully evaluate these elements in your screenplay. Be honest about how it stacks up against these tips. Make changes if you can.

365 A character who always gets his or her way because he or she is stronger, smarter, has more resources and the like needs to have a weakness or blind spot so that another character can genuinely go up against them. Every character, even an antagonist, needs an area of vulnerability.

366 Avoid easy outs for your characters. The fewer chance beneficial happenings occurring in the screenplay's second act, the stronger your story. Chance happenings can kick off a story but are better left out of the second and third acts. Coincidences and contrivances equal death to interest in a screenplay, and you lose credibility with the Hollywood Reader when you resort to these false ways to keep your story moving.

If Lulu suddenly learns she has magical powers and can easily make her boss do whatever she wants, then she doesn't have to learn, grow, and change in the story to accomplish her goal of getting promoted. Now, if Lulu learns about her ability early in the story and gets into trouble with it, that's something altogether different. Keep your character struggling. Don't provide easy outs that eliminate potential conflict.

367 If you do have a chance happening as an integral part of your story, set it up by foreshadowing it through a dream sequence or a daydream. Or have the exact same thing happen to a supporting character so it doesn't come out of left field. If you know something is going to sound like a coincidence, one way to razzle-dazzle the Hollywood Reader is to set it up. Root events in the reality of your story's universe, not in happenstance.

368 Quickly getting rid of a character around whom you've built a substantial plotline can be a waste of a great resource and may even undercut your structure. If you've invested heavily in Gwen by giving her a substantial role in many scenes, give her an equally substantial death scene and show the other characters talking about her in additional scenes. The more you integrate and interrelate the lives of the characters, the more cohesive your screenplay.

369 Monitor your characters' responses to information. If your characters regularly explode in anger, dissolve into tears, or are rendered speechless, they are losing their individuality and your story may be succumbing to melodrama. And that's a killer in the world of features.

370 Eliminate the things your characters do and say that don't in some way influence the conflict. Point everything toward complicating the conflict.

371 As you move into the third act, you should have scripted between 80 and 90 pages of your 100- to 120-page screenplay.

Script Running Long?

372 A climactic sequence needs more than just a few pages to be setup and play out, so if you're running long, don't skimp on the climax—better to cut back in Act 2 if your screenplay is running long.

Script Running Short?

373 If your feature screenplay's page count is significantly lower than 100 to 120 pages, your story may need more plot, more involved scenes, or a more complicated problem facing your protagonist. The more layers you add to a story, the more dimension and involving pages you'll have. A short script is selling itself short in terms of story and characters.

374 If your script is only ten to fifteen pages short, think about adding a new sequence in Act 2 that complicates the story and makes it difficult on your hero.

375 When you consider adding a sequence (three to five scenes), think of something that you can meld in without upsetting your entire story line.

- If your story follows a milkman falling in love with a lonely widow, add a post breakup sequence in which the milkman spends time with his ex-wife, who comes back into the picture only to realize he wants the widow.
- Add an action set piece that pumps up your hero's adrenaline going into Act 3, where he will take on his nemesis. By raising the character's adrenaline, you're raising the reader's adrenaline and pumping her up to expect conflagration in the next few pages.

376 When you offer a sequence designed to jack up the energy, weave in some inner obstacles as well so the sequence won't feel thrown in. The best way to make anything feel substantial and integral is to give it a character-grounded reason for being. Give us an emotional stake. For example, Zack has to save the secretary not because she has his Filofax but because he realizes he's in love with her. We think it's because of the Filofax, but then we (and he) realize the truth.

Your Act 2 Checklist

* *

In this second act of your screenplay, you should have done the following to beat the Hollywood Reader:

☑ Broadened your story's conflict. While there are as many ways to do this as there are stories to be told, the general principle involves showing that the issue facing the protagonist is more far-reaching than he (or we) originally supposed.

☑ So seriously complicated your protagonist's life that he is out of his own resources and is in an area of life where he has no experience from which to draw. He must change his behavior and learn new skills or fail.

- ☑ Kept the major problem your character faced in Act 1 the same but made it more intense in Act 2. If your protagonist's goal in Act 2 is now unrelated to the goal identified in Act 1, go back and make it consistent so that your story builds tension and reads as a cohesive dramatic experience.

- ☑ Continued to develop your story's subplots simultaneously with the main story line. These subplots should relate to the main story line, and their occurrence in the story line should be plotted out so that the substories develop evenly. If you've been using subplots to fill gaps or serve as commercial breaks in the script, you probably need to relate them more closely to the central story line and the central character and to integrate them more strategically throughout the script.

- ☑ Introduced all subplots and secondary characters who will participate in your story. Act 3 is too late to introduce new characters who will play an important role in your story.

- ☑ Included *at least* four major sequences in this second act. Some stories can take up to eight major sequences. If you're falling short on sequences, your story may be falling short on conflict. Rather than let that happen, go back and juice up your story.

Act 3 Goals

Finish strong! Act 3 provides your *last* chance to leave an impression with the Hollywood Reader. It can be a point of redemption if your script has flaws. Why? Most readers write up the coverage within an hour after finishing the script. A strong ending to your story can put the reader in a mood to champion your project as she basks in the glow of the fabulous third act—even if there are other problems with the script!

Sounds terribly inconsistent, doesn't it? Always remember: The Hollywood Reader is human and therefore subject to dramatic manipulation, just like the broader audience your screenplay may play to one day. Go for the gusto as you craft your story's final scenes. Have some fun and chances are your reader will enjoy the ride.

Goals to Achieve in This Third Act

★ ★

377 Use this act to show that everything that happened earlier in the story is just a preamble to the real drama.

378 Bring as many of your story's conflicts as possible to bear on your characters in this act.

379 If your story's antagonist has been disguised, reveal his/her/its identity now.

380 Put your protagonist's life, heart, happiness, or well-being in jeopardy: Everything is on the line, and there is no telling in advance *how* things will end.

381 Your protagonist's weaknesses are painfully clear now, and he should be on the way to overcoming them by ingenuity or grit or by forming an alliance with someone or something who can help.

382 Do not introduce major characters now. They will seem like contrivances and undercut the story. Integrate these characters into the first and second acts if you have not already introduced them

383 Tensions are painfully high as we near the story's climax. Characters should be at their emotional, physical, and/or psychological breaking points.

384 Pay off and resolve every plotline here. Loose ends are like ghosts that come back to haunt you.

Wowing the Reader as You Pay Off Your Story

★ ★

Act 3 is the time to pay off the story setup in the previous two acts. Conflicts come to a head as your characters are pressed to the limit in the final battle to win their goal. This is exciting stuff, so write with all the inflection you can muster to convey to the Hollywood Reader what will happen on the screen.

385 Give your story a bombshell of unexpected information at the beginning of the third act to give the Hollywood Reader another reason to keep turning the pages.

386 Cause your subplots to intersect with the central conflict in this act if they haven't already done so. If you've developed Roger's oddball family in the first two acts and have had Roger take pains to keep his fiancée from meeting the family, this is the act where you want to bring them together.

387 Have your protagonist learn yet more reasons why the antagonist must be defeated. This revelation usually involves our learning more of the truth behind the circumstances. In a romance, it means having the two characters who are in love discover that their relationship is jeopardized by a third party or by a previously well-kept secret.

388 While areas of a character's life may have been separated in previous acts, the more you now integrate them into the central conflict, the more cohesive and effective your story. An event/emotion/conflict/past action in a subplot rises to the surface in Act 3!

389 Use the third act to further raise the stakes and to give the Hollywood Reader additional reasons to invest in your protagonist. *Not only is just one infant in the hospital's nursery infected with the virus the head nurse carried, but all the other newborns in the nursery are infected as well!*

390 Bring all the protagonist's fears, previous mistakes, and personal weaknesses into play so we can measure their growth and see the content of their character. Now it's time to up the ante for your characters, making their lives and their choices tougher than ever.

Strategies That Can Help Genres Go the Distance in Act 3

Certain genres seem to fall apart in Act 3 of a feature screenplay. These tips can keep your story strong, suspenseful, and make it ultimately satisfying.

391 In a horror story, you want your evil element (the virus, the alien, the slasher) to appear unstoppable in Act 3. One very effective way to create this sense of unstoppability is by having this evil element (the antagonist) kill someone close to the protagonist, thus provoking the protagonist into an Act 3 rage. An unexpected death so late in the story can be shocking and is part of what will make your story a good example of horror.

392 In a romantic comedy, one of the best ways to keep the reader interested in the characters is to keep the lead characters apart for as long as possible. When the characters get together in a romantic comedy in which conflict has thrived on keeping them apart through misunderstanding and immaturity, the story is over—the two are together and so have overcome the obstacles that separated them. Don't unite your characters too soon. Keep them separate to keep your reader interested.

393 In a family drama, the third act (and the climactic sequence in particular) needs to prove that the family has grown since Acts 1 and 2. Take the family from their lowest point in Act 2, create a new situation that threatens the household or someone in it, and force the family members into talking with each other. Act 3 provides the final test of this family so that when it looks as though all is lost for them, they're able to pull together, to overcome their pride and hurt and work as a team for the survival of one of their members.

Climax

394 This is it! The climax provides the final confrontation between the protagonist and the antagonist. It's where your protagonist engages in the final battle to win his goal. It's what we've been waiting for—make it worth the wait!

The agoraphobic must save his girlfriend from the Mustache Twirler, who holds her atop the Empire State Building.

Toss in every conflict you've created at this point. A strong climax makes use of subplots, which come to bear on this intense moment of action. The protagonist won't face the antagonist again, so play out this sequence with some passion.

395 The climactic sequence can take up to twenty pages of action, but the stakes have to accelerate and the situation become more complicated if it's going to hold our interest. You cannot sustain a single note during twenty pages. Think of the last minutes of *Rocky*, when our underdog boxer goes for it in the ring. That's a climax that works, filled with peaks and valleys that keep us on the edge of our seats. That's what you have to work for if you want to go the distance in an extended climactic sequence.

396 Steer clear of clichés in the climactic sequence. In the wake of *Fatal Attraction*, many thrillers had an apparently dead antagonist suddenly springing back to life and threatening the protagonist yet again. Be original.

397 Put at stake what your character wants most: the relationship, the athletic title, the fate of the universe. If the character doesn't really want it, don't build a climax around it—it won't work.

398 Use everything the protagonist has learned in the story to resolve the central conflict. The more new knowledge or abilities he uses, the more you show that the character has been growing and transforming.

399 Bring your protagonist face-to-face with the antagonist during the climax to generate some sweat. Intermediaries dilute the suspense and tension.

400 When you do bring the protagonist and antagonist together for their final battle, do so in a way that doesn't seem accidental. Having the two bump into each other in the subway or discovering that they're part of the same tour group in the Middle East can make your story seem haphazard. Put some thought into what will bring the two together, and make the meeting an exciting, suspenseful process that builds exquisite tension as we move into the climax.

401 As you decide the location of your climactic sequence, consider returning the protagonist to the place or event that launched him into the conflict. For example, if a teen sees his cop dad gunned down in a field, we know the teen has come full circle when he avenges his dad's death in the same field. But now, as a result of the events the teen endured during the story, we know he is a man rather than the boy he was when he saw the murder. Bringing a character back to the scene of the crime that spurred the story into motion adds symbolism and is an organic way to make backstory meaningful.

402 The protagonist must stand to lose something in the climactic sequence. His life, his love, everything that he stands for—you get the idea.

403 Make the act of resolving the conflict intensely personal for your characters.

> *Not only does Susan have to save the world, but she must prove to herself that she doesn't fall apart when the pressure is on.*

404 Keep your protagonist consistent as he solves the central conflict. If Melvin has never before fired a gun, make him clumsy as he takes a shot at the antagonist in the climax. Nothing can undercut credibility like a protagonist who suddenly becomes competent. He may as well become another person!

The Climactic Set Piece

405 In an action screenplay, the climactic set piece needs to be the biggest, most exciting, most original action sequence in the screenplay. A huge car pileup is not an acceptable climactic set piece.

The Climax in a Relationship Drama

406 In a relationship drama, put everything on the line as the characters verbally spar at a new level of honesty. The point is to shake the internal universes of these characters in the same way that you want to shake the external universe when nuclear weapon–toting thugs go at it in the climax of an action story.

Keep Your Story Smart

407 Keep your story smart enough so that the characters have to dig for the solutions to their problems. Stories betray weakness when they suddenly offer a simple resolution, begging the question, "Why didn't the character think of that in the first place?" If detective Johnson questions everyone but the eyewitness about the murder, then finally questions that witness in Act 3 and is led straight to the killer, the result is not a satisfying payoff to the mystery.

Characters and the Climax

408 Keep your antagonist smart during the climax. A smart antagonist forces the protagonist to go to new levels in the final combat. A dumb antagonist is not a worthy opponent and doesn't raise the stakes like a smart opponent can.

409 Keep your characters consistent throughout the climactic sequence. If Marty is a less-than-smart bumbler, make it a fluke that he resolves the central conflict. Don't suddenly make dumb characters smart, bumbling characters savvy, and unlucky characters lucky to rescue them from their problems.

410 Avoid providing your protagonist an unrealistic window of opportunity to get the upper hand in the battle with the antagonist. The antagonist holding a gun to your protagonist's head, then going into an extended explanation of his or her actions and unwittingly allowing the protagonist to get free, is an easy and all-too-common resolution.

411 Play it straight at the climax. Ditch any plot point that has even a whiff of contrivance or coincidence—you risk undermining the reader's opinion of your whole story. For example, extricating Buddy from debt by his winning the lottery, giving Owen psychic powers at the last moment so he can get out of trouble—these choices read as cheating. Don't cheat your climax, characters, or script.

Does the Protagonist Need to Succeed?

412 The protagonist needs to experience a measure of victory in the climactic sequence for the story to be satisfying. John may not save the relationship, but he learned the truth and saved himself years of heartache in the future. Whitney may not win the race, but she arrived at the contest and finished, proving something to herself (and to us) in the process.

It's Do or Die for Your Characters

★ ★

Now is the time to show the Hollywood Reader the stuff your characters are made of. Use these tips as a guide while putting your characters through the toughest times of their lives. These tips will keep your characters on track and serving your story.

Speaking of story . . . If you've been having some trouble with your story, you might just find that if you apply these tips to your characters, your story problems will resolve themselves in Act 3. The root of story problems is often the characters.

Protagonist

413 Keep the protagonist appealing throughout the conflict, even though his weaknesses are showing.

414 Press the protagonist beyond his limit. The protagonist should have to use newfound reserves of strength, newly discovered talents for achieving his goal. If your protagonist could have resolved the conflict in the opening act, he hasn't been growing and changing enough.

415 Visually show your protagonist's transformation in the final scenes of the screenplay. Show us the new ability to overcome fear of heights, the new courage to tell the truth, the new tenacity that enables him to persevere when earlier in the story he would have given up and walked away when the going got tough.

Antagonist

416 Now is the time to reveal your antagonist's true nature, if you haven't already done so.

417 Your antagonist should be opposing your protagonist with everything at his disposal.

418 This is the time that your antagonist's weakness or flaw can be exposed without undermining the plot. The revelation gives your protagonist a way to win in battle. One caution: Be sure that this revelation is not something that could have been identified earlier in the story and saved the protagonist a great deal of trouble. If that is the case, it can make your whole story seem ridiculously contrived and shamelessly manipulative.

All Characters

419 Make everything you've developed about your characters work in this act—their appearance, stature, education, ethnicity. If the detail doesn't have a bearing here, it may not be worth including in the screenplay.

Final Character Transformation

420 Act 3 offers the final opportunity to reveal what each and every personality you've created is made of.

421 Make the events of the story affect the characters—either positively or negatively. Characters who go through the motions of the story without changing at all need alterations.

422 If the protagonist's actions and decisions do not impact the other characters, rethink your protagonist. He needs to be able to create a ripple effect on the people around him.

423 While you want to keep character transformation in the realm of the plausible, remember that the greater the transformation, the stronger the potential response to your project.

424 Transform your characters' physical liabilities into benefits in this act—a midget utilizes his size to elude his pursuers, for example.

Character Relationships

425 The relationships between characters undergo a final shift in the climactic sequence. Minds and hearts should change once and for all. Either Margaret loves Don or she doesn't. Either Steve wants the job or he doesn't.

The Kind of End That Can Get You a Reader Recommend

★ ★

Some writers say that finding the right ending for their story is the toughest part of a screenplay. Try some different endings, see how these play to friends when you pitch them your story in conversation, then take the ending that elicits the response you're going for. No matter what ending you choose, check it against these tips to make it as strong as it can be.

The Screenplay's Conclusion

426 All endings should move us in some way so that we come away with a feeling that this is a story worth telling. The last scenes are a bell. Use them to hit the notes that pay off your story most appropriately.

427 Be true to your tale as you craft its conclusion. If your script tells a bleak story, a sweet conclusion will seem artificial. *Leaving Las Vegas* struck a note with audiences because of its unflinching honesty all the way through to the end.

428 A conclusion can surprise but must hold together in terms of the story. If aliens rescue Mimi and Ted at the last minute, but aliens have not been a part of the story (on or off screen) in previous acts, this is not a convincing way to end.

429 Not every story can end happily, but all stories should be satisfying. Tammy doesn't manage to snag Brent, but she knows herself better as a result of pursuing him and dealing with rejection. Character growth is usually one of the most powerful elements that contribute to a satisfying ending.

430 If you create an *up ending*, make sure this ending is not artificial and happy just because you want to end the story with a smile. Not all stories can end well and still maintain their integrity.

431 It is possible to end your story on a scary note and still satisfy the audience that your story was worth telling. The immediate conflict may be over but the character has lost in terms of the big picture.

- *Sylvia saves her family from the plague, but unseen by her a rat runs into the house* [and we know that rats spread this plague].
- *The survivors of a horrible siege stand at the grave site of those who terrorized them, not realizing that the leader of the terrorist group is among their number.*

These kinds of endings are especially appropriate if you're setting up a sequel or a springboard for a television series.

432 When you choose an ironic ending, be sure that the process the protagonist goes through is interesting enough to make the story worth telling.

Herbert spends the story searching for and finding the buried treasure he needs in order to win Victoria's heart, only to return home to find Victoria in love with a penniless suitor.

If we've enjoyed adventures with Herbert as he searches for the treasure, and if Herbert has learned life-changing things about himself along the way, then an ironic ending can satisfy. However, if you choose a *Twilight Zone*–like ironic ending and close on confusion, outrage, or some similar negative emotion, your story may seem contrived and unsatisfying.

433 The ending can be tragic but such an ending must fit the story and be the only solution to the protagonist's problem. While *Leaving Las Vegas* offers a tragic conclusion, the story also includes an up note with the promise that the prostitute is moving on in her own life as a result of her encounter with the alcoholic.

434 Concerned your resolution is vague and undefined? The good news is that today's endings don't need to be neat and tidy. It's okay to show a relationship still evolving, but do reveal the characters' emotional and mental growth.

435 No matter what ending you choose, keep this conclusion in the same tone as the rest of the story. A fluffy romantic comedy that kills off its leads at the conclusion will befuddle the Hollywood Reader.

436 If at all possible, end with the focus on your main characters to show that you understand who and what your story was about.

437 If your protagonist is dead, end with a tribute to him.

438 While you can show the toll that resolving the central conflict took on your protagonist, let us know that the process was worthwhile for him.

Where to End Your Story

439 End your story a scene or two after the climax concludes so we can see life getting back to normal for the protagonist.

440 The exception to this is if you freeze the camera and offer a voice-over:

> *In 1984, Congress passed legislation in response to this horrible crime, calling it Judy's Law.*

If you want to have words appear on the screen, write the word *CRAWL* and then the information you want.

CRAWL:

```
One in two marriages will break up before reaching
the third anniversary.
```

The Denouement

441 A screenplay's final scenes after the climactic sequence should show that your protagonist finally has what he has been fighting for.

- If Guy dreams of opening a bar on a tropical island, end with his making a piña colada on this island.
- If Sam has been chasing Tina in an attempt to get her to marry him, end on their wedding day.

442 Including more than five pages of denouement suggests the story is too long, the climax is misplaced, or that you are overwriting.

443 Briefly show a new opportunity opening up for the characters, dramatizing that their life goes on. But keep these scenes lean, lest you begin telling another story instead of ending the one you started.

A last scene provides your final opportunity to make an impression on the Hollywood Reader and your audience. It is the final emotion before the credits roll. Choose it with care.

444 The more clear a connection you can make between your opening and final scenes, the more cohesive your screenplay.

445 The final scene is the place to restore what's been lost in the first act. Lost love is found again, stolen treasure is recovered and put back into the right hands, the scales of justice tip back into balance.

446 The most effective final scenes set the story into its larger context and make a connection between the story, life, and the world.

447 If you asked a question in the opening sequence, answer it here (if you haven't already).

448 If you opened the screenplay with a voice-over, end the screenplay with voice-over to give a sense of continuity.

449 If the words "The End" occur on page 99 (or earlier), chances are you need to tell a more complex story. Add one more sequence for rhythm and conflict, and to jack up the stakes. Writing a short script is giving yourself short shrift in the entertainment game.

450 Uncomfortable with your conclusion? Try a different ending and see how the story plays to friends.

Your Act 3 Checklist

★ ★

In this third act of your screenplay, you should have done the following to beat the Hollywood Reader:

☑ Used the scenes in this act to show that everything in Acts 1 and 2 were just a prelude to the *real* drama. In other words, you've made this final act something worth waiting for, and you haven't disappointed us. You really *did* save the best for last.

☑ Brought all (or most of) the conflicts developed earlier in your story to bear on your characters in this act.

☑ Revealed your antagonist's identity in this act if you kept it hidden during Acts 1 and 2.

☑ Put your protagonist's life, heart, or happiness in jeopardy in this act, and you kept the outcome a suspenseful secret until the final moment of the act.

☑ Showed your protagonist's weaknesses to be painfully apparent in this act and how he had to overcome these by ingenuity, sheer grit, or by forming an alliance with someone or something who could help him. There's no way your protagonist could have engaged successfully in the final conflict using only the resources he possessed at the story's opening.

☑ Made sure the tensions were at their highest going into this act and especially going into the climax.

☑ Pushed your characters to their emotional, physical, and/or psychological breaking points during this act.

☑ Resolved every conflict introduced earlier in your story by the time you wrote FADE OUT.

Correct Common Flaws Related to Genre

★ ★

Certain genres require special attention. These tips address the flaws that most often undermine popular genres and make recommending genre pieces impossible for the typical Hollywood Reader.

Hot Tips For Every Genre

451 Reveal your genre from page 1 and be consistent.
- A rollicking actioner needs action right away.
- A moody character drama needs mood and a setup for drama, not a wild car chase that makes the rest of your story seem slow by comparison.

452 When you mix genres (mixing comedy with horror, for example), establish a tone and stick with it. Adding a gruesome murder to an otherwise lighthearted romantic comedy will seem out of place.

Relationships and Genre

453 Whatever genre you explore, place an important relationship at stake as the action unfolds. This will help draw the interest of a Hollywood Reader who may be disinclined toward the genre (the comedy-loving Hollywood Reader assigned to cover a hardware-heavy actioner, for example). Doing this can also strengthen your story and characters, making your screenplay more attractive to top actors searching for complex roles in commercial screenplays.

The Historical Genre

454 Avoid being just another costume drama. Explore issues if you expect a studio to invest millions in bringing your story to the screen.

455 If your screenplay is a biography, decide on an emphasis. Showcase a dangerous friendship, a deception that marked the character's life but which is only now coming to light, or give it an emphasis which previous historians have not. *Jefferson in Paris* does the latter as it explores the love of Thomas Jefferson and Sally Hemmings. If you have nothing new to bring to the story of a historical personality, reconsider the subject matter and explore a topic on which you can shed new light.

456 When choosing a period story, keep the age of your target audience in mind. If the audience knows nothing about that era, if the era doesn't resonate romance or intrigue or style, it may require more setup than a story set in an era about which the audience is familiar. The Korean War doesn't have the cinematic romance that World War II has, because people know more about the latter.

457 Differentiate your true-life historical drama from a history lesson. While it is unwise to *ignore* the facts, don't be a slave to fact or feel that you must tell the audience every detail. Documentaries inform; the goal of entertainment is to entertain. That audiences sometimes receive valuable information from feature movies is a bonus.

458 If you're considering a historically based drama, be sure to tell a story rather than describe an incident. An incident is a single event; a story consists of a series of incidents that builds a total dramatic experience with a clear beginning, middle, and end.

In creating a story about a famous explosion that decimates the citizens of a town, describe the last day or days in the lives of the people living in that town at the time of the explosion. Show couples falling in love, children at school, promises being made, dreams being hatched, and more—build a story around the incident so that the ultimate explosion has an effect that provokes a strong response in us. *Titanic* does this beautifully as it builds a larger-than-life romance aboard a doomed ship.

459 As you craft your historical piece, beware of hinging your plot on anachronisms that can undermine your story's authenticity. A thriller set in the 1870s will not ring true if the plot hinges on Victoria phoning a friend for help.

460 Historically based pieces must tap into the universal experience so the story is relevant to the contemporary Hollywood Reader. Accomplish this by highlighting the struggles the characters face in their relationships, with their enemies, and within themselves. *Titanic* is a story about people coping with classism and learning to captain their own destiny as much as it is a story about a ship sinking.

461 Build around contemporary events or technology. If you're using the Cuban missile crisis as the basis for your screenplay's conflict, you might want to reconsider your story. It's tough to sell executives on stories involving old news unless you add a relevant contemporary spin.

462 Thrillers need a strong human element to heighten the conflict and to prove that you've created more than a series of intricate plot twists. Like the audience your movie will eventually play to, the Hollywood Reader ultimately roots for characters, so you must create characters appealing and interesting enough to root for.

463 Make the technology in your techno or military thriller accessible and understandable to a low-tech Hollywood Reader. Take pains to create modest descriptions of advanced weaponry that a person who is not into weaponry can understand, laying out in simple terms how the weapon functions, what it can do, why it is so threatening.

> *The Stealth Bomber: silent, hovers like a hummingbird, deadly.*

The idea is to describe the qualities and capabilities of the technology you will be using in the story. If certain capabilities of the machinery won't come into play, there is probably no need to detail them. What you want to avoid are overly involved descriptions that confuse more than illuminate. Keep it brief, keep it relevant.

464 In a romance, characters need to think about more than love for your story to carry weight. Provide your characters with lives that make them seem real enough so that romance is just *part* of their world. Give your characters jobs, homes, families, pasts, likes, and dislikes.

465 Most romances need more than hit-and-run romantic encounters between characters to hold the interest of the Hollywood Reader. Create significant scenes involving the central couple in the story. While the two may not spend a great deal of time together in the first act, show them communicating in some way that builds audience belief that these two people belong together. While *Sleepless in Seattle* waits until the conclusion to put its lovers together on screen, the piece offers significant scenes convincing us that these two people belong together. That's what you should shoot for.

466 If you do create a romance around casual encounters, these encounters must create a profound connection between the characters, one which cannot be dismissed easily and which is ultimately worth building a story around.

467 Romances are fueled by ever-deepening levels of intimacy and trust between the two characters involved. For the encounters to seem profound, characters must trade information they learn about each other, their circumstances, and themselves, and then act on it as they attempt to integrate it into their lives.

For example, Betty mentions that Rick looks different (he's gained twenty pounds). That casual comment propels Rick into a fitness regimen that includes joining a gym, eating health food, and limiting himself to beer only on Saturday nights. Betty is having an effect on Rick.

Concerning Love Scenes

468 Love scenes are supposed to turn us on, not gross us out. Emulating the butter scene in *Last Tango in Paris* or the food sex scene from *9½ Weeks* could leave you with something that's simply disgusting.

Action

469 A big-budget actioner needs a *very* strong reason for us to root for the protagonist before the action will have impact and make sense. The protagonist risking all to save lives, secure love, or make the world a safe, happy place to live are a few general ways to get us behind him. The point is to create a scenario in which your protagonist pursues a clear goal with distinct, horrific penalties for failure (death, losing out on love forever, a tyrant running the world).

470 Creating a unique hero can enhance the chances of your actioner getting recommended, especially to top talent. Giving your hero a physical disability (deafness), an emotional disability (fear of losing another loved one), or a tragic past (wrongful imprisonment for twenty years) are a few ways to create an unusual component to a heroic character while simultaneously adding depth to your story.

Children and Family

471 When writing for a family audience, respect the kids and parents you target by formulating sophisticated characters and a *smart* story. The smarter your concept and story, the broader the audience you will attract in the family/mainstream arena.

472 Create three-dimensional characters with aspirations, emotional complexity, relationships that aren't always easy, and conflicts that take more than one or two steps to resolve. The more dimensions you build into your characters, the more memorable and possibly enduring your characters will be. While Mary Poppins is a make-believe character with the ability to perform magic, she has a complexity that allows her to lose her temper, state her opinion, show a streak of vanity, and generally enjoy a wide range of emotions.

473 To ensure that your children's screenplay makes it past the Hollywood Reader, create a concept kids can understand. Mom and Dad's sexual dysfunction will not be something five-year-olds comprehend, while Mom and Dad's general unhappiness will be something that younger kids *can* key into.

474 While Hollywood has a thing for the smart kid/dumb adult paradigm, the best stories have the children *and* adults learning and growing. An added benefit to following this tip is that when the adults in the story change, you broaden the story's scope and create the possibility of drawing a larger audience, which is something that the Hollywood Reader looks for. In *Mary Poppins*, each member of the Banks family changes as a result their unusual nanny's influence.

475 Know what matters to children at various ages, and create stories that explore these issues.

476 Viable family entertainment sidesteps adult humor, profanity, and graphic violence. Work around these elements when formulating your concept, story, and characters to create a script that genuinely appeals to a younger audience.

477 Producers of children's films look for screenplays that explore themes like the importance of telling the truth, obeying parents, and sharing. Building a story around themes like these can increase the chances of your screenplay getting recommended.

Part 3

***

Epilogue

Feedback-Driven Revision

(It's the shortest path to a better script)

* *

Congratulations! You've written a screenplay designed to beat the Hollywood Reader and are ready to send photocopies around town.

But hold everything! Before sending your baby into shark-infested Hollywood, here are a few more tips to consider.

478 Show your screenplay to trusted friends and colleagues who watch television, see movies, and are in touch with popular culture. Listen to what they say. There is no better judge of how successfully you've tapped into the moviegoing experience than by running your story by the average moviegoer.

479 Revise any weaknesses that two or more people note. When two people say there's a problem, there's a problem.

480 Save professional contacts for later drafts, when your work is more polished. Consider this: You have only one chance to show your project to someone for the first time. First impressions endure, so make those first impressions as strong as possible.

481 Use the process of feedback-driven revision for as long as it takes to get a story that satisfies. Consult your peanut gallery, revise your story, then rerun the process. When your group of nonprofessional Hollywood Readers can no longer agree on the screenplay's flaws, chances are you're ready to face the professional Hollywood Reader.

482 Register your screenplay with the WGA-w or WGA-e (Writer's Guild of America west and east). For a nominal fee, your project will be registered as proof that the concept, characters, and story are yours. If you plan to show your work around Hollywood, it makes sense to guard yourself against possible theft of your ideas. The stakes are as high as the ambitions of the players. Protect yourself. Call the WGA-w in Los Angeles at 323-951-4000 for more information.

483 Be willing to make the changes a company may require if they buy your property. Screenplays often become group projects when they go in for further development after purchase. Development executives, directors, even stars have ideas for altering the story and characters. Get used to the idea of people changing your work. That's show biz!

Still Didn't Get Positive Coverage?

★ ★

Rejection is part of the Hollywood game. If your screenplay is on the receiving end of this rejection, keep a stiff upper lip. It's not over until you say it's over.

Take to heart as many of these tips as you can and send your screenplay out again. These changes will alter those characteristics of a project that most companies check for when scanning their files for previous coverage.

There is more than one way to beat a Hollywood Reader!

Take it from a veteran who has changed her mind about a project or two.

484 Give your screenplay a new title.

485 If you have an old date or draft number on the script, remove it. Draft numbers and dates don't belong on script covers unless the script is currently in development.

486 Use a pseudonym.

487 Change the screenplay's page count. Some companies check for previous coverage and will only permit new coverage if the screenplay contains a different number of pages than the previous draft.

488 Change the names of the lead characters.

489 Alter the screenplay's opening and closing sequences.

490 Update key elements in your screenplay so the project reflects cutting-edge issues.

491 Change the ages of the characters to change the Hollywood Reader's perception of the story and the intensity of the conflicts.

492 Flip the genders of your characters to give the story a new feel. Make the dangerous serial killer a woman, for example.

493 Set your story in a different century to change the genre.

494 Strengthen a few key areas of your screenplay to make it a stronger example of the genre. Add more action sequences to your actioner, and make the action more original.

495 Give your story a new hook.

496 Eliminate unnecessary scenes or sequences.

497 Play up key elements in your project so the material hooks into a genre that's currently riding a wave of popularity.

498 Change aspects of your key characters—make your banker a lumberjack, your homemaker a rocket scientist.

499 Submit a polished draft of the screenplay. A fully developed screenplay is a necessity if you want your work accepted by a Hollywood Reader. While it is true that concepts sell in Hollywood, well-written screenplays sell for much more.

Jennifer Lerch

500 If nobody is interested in the screenplay, write another one. When there's interest in the second screenplay, the studio will want to know what else you've got—and you just might sell the first screenplay along with the second screenplay. It happens all the time.

Conclusion

★ ★

There's nothing mysterious about beating the Hollywood Reader. Tell a good story while adhering to standard screenplay format. Get feedback to see if the words on the page effectively convey your vision. Make necessary corrections. Then watch the Hollywood Reader scramble to get positive coverage onto the executive's desk.

Beat the Hollywood Reader by writing the screenplay the Hollywood Reader wants to recommend.

Hollywood needs more stories. Be the one to write them.

Then tell me about it at Ways500@aol.com.